God is Good All-Ways and Always!

By

Donna Watson

Dedication

I dedicate this book to Jesus Christ, my Lord and Savior. I give God the glory for inspiring me to write it because of the blessed life that I have learned to live from His teachings in the Holy Bible. I have learned that God is good always and all ways!

I also dedicate this book to my family; they mean the world to me and are a big reason that I wrote this book. I wanted to teach my family and anyone who reads this book that accepting Jesus as your Savior gives you more than a ticket to heaven when you die. You are given power to live an abundant life on earth.

Table of Contents

INTRODUCTION

If there is one thing that I have learned and that everyone must realize is that in our universe there is a higher force at work. There are actually two forces at work, one being good and the other one being evil. The good one, God, has defeated the evil one, Satan.

When I was very young, I didn't understand the push and pull in our spirits. God was calling me to him, and the devil was trying to stop me from following God.

It was a bit of a tug of war that everyone goes through, and our choices define who we are and how we live this life.

God gives us free will to choose how we will live. He doesn't force himself on us, but he wants us to choose to love him and to have a relationship with him.

Because you know what? God loved us first, and no matter what you have done, God loves you, and he wants to be in your life. He wants you to become his child through his precious son Jesus.

His whole purpose for creating you was for you to have a connection with him on a daily basis. He loves you more than you know or comprehend.

I used to believe a lie about God, that he was more or less a tyrant. That is so far from the truth, and I know now that God is good all ways and always!

I want to thank you for reading my book. I have wanted to write it for a long time.

I prayed to God for guidance in writing this book. I believe he has inspired me to write it, to teach you what I have learned through my relationship with him and divine revelation from his word, the Holy Bible.

My heart's desire is that this book helps you in some way because I have shared a few of my life experiences and my testimonies.

You will see that I am just a regular person. I'm nothing on my own. I draw my strength from God through his precious son Jesus.

It's amazing what God has done for me, and he will do the same thing for you if you believe. I hope this book blesses you.

I hope that after you read it, you decide that you want to have a deeper relationship with God through Jesus. That will be a tremendous blessing to me also.

CHAPTER 1

About me

I am a server. I have spent my life serving others and doing whatever I needed to please them.

It was instilled in me from God from my beginning. I find extreme pleasure in helping others.

If I Know that I can make a difference in someone else's life I will do it.

I have been that way my whole life. I know that it came from God, and I thank him for making me that way because my servitude has blessed others and myself throughout the years.

I was born into a low-income family in the 60s. I didn't say poor, but by other people's standards we were poor.

I didn't notice it that much because that's the only way of life that I knew.

Other extended family members lived the same way that we did.

So, we didn't have any other way of life to compare ours to.

I didn't see what being rich was like except through a couple of classmates. I had an occasion or two to see their houses and realized that our little wood house did not compare.

I knew from interaction at school that our clothes did not compare, but that was not a problem for me.

I am not a designer kind of person. I am very simple, and in clothing and shoes, I go for comfort. Lol!

As far as my friends were concerned. I really don't know that they were rich, but they definitely lived in a better house than we did.

Of course, we didn't live in the same little house my whole life, but no matter what address we had, the little house didn't change.

My mom always made our little house a home. It was clean and tidy. She loved whatnots and throw rugs, and it showed.

God is Good
All-Ways and Always!

***

Nothing matched, but she made it all come together so nicely. Our curtains may have been the latest plastic design, but we always had colorful ones.

To me, it was all so beautifully decorated. I was happy walking in and seeing all of the things that she loved.

I would call her style country eclectic. I didn't know that term at the time, but it means decorating with anything that you love.

Decorating with what you can afford and not worrying about what anyone else thinks. Lol!

My mom had a knack for it. Our house was always cozy and inviting.

My mom was very particular with the house. We took our shoes off at the door, and we never sat on the furniture. After our baths, we could sit on the couch, but it always had a cover over it.

There was one chair that we were never allowed to sit in. It was a French provincial style; that's what Mama called it.

It was off-limits! In fact, after she died, we were still afraid to sit in that chair. I don't think she ever sat in it either; it was just for looking at! Lol.

Our little houses were always 2 bedrooms and 1 bath. Old wood windows that you couldn't open because they were warped from years of shrinking and swelling due to temperature changes.

All five rooms were always so small and not functional for their purpose.

Two bedrooms, one bath, kitchen, and living and dining room together in about 1000 sq. ft. or less.

We didn't have heat or air other than a space heater and a box fan. So in wintertime you were freezing, and in summer you were hot as a firecracker!

You could feel the wind blowing through the cracks in the walls in the wintertime.

You did not even need refrigeration for your food because it was so cold on some of those days.

In the summertime there was never a good breeze to relieve the stifling nights. It was horrible; you lay there sweating and hoping you could just fall asleep so that you wouldn't be aware of how miserable you were.

We didn't stay inside during the daytime, so the temperature didn't matter then. It only mattered at night when we had to lie down to rest because then you noticed how uncomfortable it was.

You notice I said we had to lie down to rest? That's because we would have stayed outside all day and night if they had let us!

***

You know kids have long-lasting energy, and sitting still or resting is like torture. Especially for us, we had so many things that we wanted to do and the days were never long enough.

To the north of our house was a hardware store. They always had huge cardboard boxes discarded out back from appliance deliveries.

They were perfect for building forts and houses.

We would connect 3 or 4 together and have a multi-room mansion.

When we were done playing in our cardboard mansions.

We would break them down and lay them on a small hill beside our house. We had a ski slope then.

We would slide down with our socks on or roll and tumble end over end. We had hours of fun!

Our dad had brought a big wooden spool home one day. The kind that large electrical wire was wrapped around.

We became circus actors, and we walked that spool down the hill and across the yard. We lay down, and the other one walked over you. What a thrill! We played with that spool for years.

Although we lived in the city, we could always find adventure somewhere.

The shopping center was right across the street. You could walk 30 ft from our house and be in the parking lot.

Back in that day, soda bottles had a deposit to return them to the store. People discarded their bottles in ditches along the road, throwing them out of their car windows.

That was a jackpot for us. We would walk around gathering as many as we could, and we would take them to the store to cash them in. With the cash, we could buy a drink and a bag full of penny candy. Yes, candy was a penny back then. Individually wrapped and every kind of candy imaginable!

God is Good
All-Ways and Always!

I loved living in our little house in our little town because although it was a small town, it was busy.

We knew everyone entering and leaving the shopping center back then.

We would sit on our little wooden porch and wave to all of the people entering and leaving the parking lot throughout the day.

***

After hours and on Sundays, the parking lot was a huge asphalt playground for us when all of the stores closed.

That actually used to be a thing; businesses closed on Sundays and holidays. You had to have your shopping done by Saturday, or it would have to wait until Monday.

People took time out to be with the family and to go to church.

The city shut down except for maybe a gas station for travelers, and I think they may have opened after church.

We could ride our bikes or skateboards all over the parking lot on those days without any danger of being hit by a car. We had our own asphalt sports park, and it was free.

I could tell stories of the multiple times that we got road rash in that parking lot!

Well, it was mainly me; my brother was always more in control of what he was doing. I've always been a little bit of a klutz and easily injured.

I don't know, maybe it was because I would always get more excited than him.

I would run head-on into something, and he would always think it through before doing it.

I know that was the wisest thing now, but I didn't think about the end result at the time. I was going to try that stunt even if it killed me. Well, I have the scars to prove it! Lol.

I am still an excitable person.

I have learned to curb it with age so that on the outside I look calm and collected. On the inside I'm still that excited little kid ready to run straight into the world.

We lived by the railroad tracks for a big part of my life, and I considered that a fringe benefit. I loved to hear the train whistle blow and watch the cars rushing by. It always gave me a sense of excitement!

Just thinking about that large piece of machinery traveling so fast and going to places I had never seen gave me such pleasure.

Then there were also the times we would put coins and things on the tracks to see what would happen when the train ran over them.

***

I would anxiously await the train and pray that it wouldn't derail because we had placed an item on the track.

My brother, who I viewed as someone like Einstein because he was smarter than me and understood how things worked. He would convince me that the train might derail, so be ready to run just in case!

I would sit there in bated fear, waiting and regretting placing a coin or other item on the tracks.

Yes, I am that gullible, and no matter how many times he was wrong, the train would just crush the item or push it off of the track. I would still believe him the next time.

Living by the tracks had a negative connotation, but not to me. Other people may have had nicer homes in nicer areas than us, but they didn't have the railroad tracks!

I was completely happy there, and I miss hearing and seeing the train even today.

It was just the two of us growing up, my brother and me. We were like two peas in a pod. He is 18 months older than me. If you were to ever meet him, he would tell you that I am the oldest, but that's not true; it's just his way of picking on me. He's always known how to push my buttons.

I didn't realize earlier that I could have stopped him if I hadn't let him get to me.

He would pick and pick until I was angry. It took a lot because I have the longest fuse of anyone that I know, but when it finally goes.

I believe that I get angrier than most. It would probably have been best to let the steam out before that point because sometimes my temper went a little crazy! If you knew me, you wouldn't believe it, but it is true: I have chased him with a shovel, a hoe, and a knife before, I am sorry to admit! Lol.

God is Good
All-Ways and Always!

I really can't stand conflict, and I don't like being angry. I'm so upset if I think someone is mad at me. God made me to love people, and I do. In my heart I believe that there is good in everyone, and I look for that. I am quick to forgive people because I want others to forgive me too.

We had a lot of good times, and we relied on each other a lot. We have a bond as siblings that's hard to break. Even if we don't see each other regularly, the bond is still there.

We endured some things as children that are unspoken. They will remain that way, but through it all we drew closer together. Thank God we had each other through those years.

***

We never had our own bedroom because of the little two-bedroom houses that we lived in. Our belongings were in the same room. My brother would have a couple of dresser drawers for his clothes, and I had a couple for mine.

Our hanging clothes were on a makeshift bar for a closet. Our toys are separated and organized neatly in the corner. The room was always neat and clean.

We only had one little bed in the room, so we took turns sleeping on the couch. We didn't mind that at all actually because if you were the one who got the couch, it was almost like you didn't have to go to bed. It felt special and fun.

***

I can remember almost every Christmas gift that I ever received because there were not that many. It was enough though; we were always happy with what we got.

There was only one year that we noticed that things were different. The only thing that we got was a board game called Clue. We didn't cry and complain; we didn't know why there wasn't more, but it wasn't our place to ask either. We didn't want to cause more pain and grief to our parents.

We had hours of fun playing that game!

When I married, I still had every doll that I had ever gotten. All of them looked immaculate. We took care of our things because they didn't come easily.

We used to play with all of the neighborhood kids in the afternoon. We gathered at the edge of the public cemetery. There was an open field that didn't have any graves yet.

God is Good
All-Ways and Always!

It was almost like The Sandlot; we all just gathered to play the game. It might be baseball, football, or soccer. It was just understood that we would gather at the field.

We would sometimes go to our house because we were lucky enough to have a basketball goal hung on the side of an old barn behind our house.

***

When the streetlights came on, we had better be home. It was time for baths and supper.

After supper we were allowed to watch TV until 9pm, no later. If there was anything worth watching.

We had an outside antenna for reception. If you were lucky, you could get 1 or 2 channels to tune in. Someone had to literally go outside and turn the antenna until the television picture came in clearly.

Our dad would sit inside and holler instructions until the picture was clear. When it came in clearly and you let go of the antenna pole, the picture would scramble most of the time, and you would have to start over.

It didn't matter if it was cold or raining; the antenna had to be tweaked or there wouldn't be any television that night.

I remember the first color television that we got. The colors were amazing!

The very first TV show that I remember seeing was I Dream of Jeannie. Her outfit was so beautiful in color; I did not imagine it that way when we were watching in black and white. I can still remember how beautiful it was to this day.

We lived in a carefree time in history. The 60s and 70s were safer times. Kids could walk down the streets and not be afraid. I never heard of anyone being kidnapped until Ted Bundy took Kimberly Leach in Lake City, FL, in 1978. An hour away from our home.

Up until then I had no idea that people like him existed or that being kidnapped was a possibility and I was 15 years old.

Overall, we had as good of a life as possible growing up. We were fed and clothed the best that our parents could afford.

Our mom was a good person; she always had a smile on her face. She always kept our home neat and clean. Our clothes were clean and tidy. She made sure that we had food on the table. She prepared so many delicious meals, but a few stand out to me.

On cold winter nights there would be a pot of the most delicious soup with beef, potatoes, and vegetables. Homemade cornbread with mayonnaise to put on top (don't knock it until you try it); it's a family tradition from my granny. It's delicious!

We would sit at our little table, and that soup would fill our bellies and make us warm. I couldn't have asked for a better meal. At that time in my mind, we were the richest people on earth.

***

Our dad was different. He worked a lot, and we preferred it that way. We were uneasy when he was around. He was not usually in a good mood. We had no idea at the time, but it was because he was an addict. That was brought to light later from his own admissions. We knew something was wrong, but we could never figure it out. Our parents hid it well.

My dad's life was hard as a child, and he carried all of the demons from his past into adulthood. I don't believe he knew what love was until he met my mom. He wasn't the best dad while we were growing up, but I forgave him. He did accept Jesus as his savior, and he tried to escape his past, but he never came to realize everything that Jesus did for him, so he didn't have true peace throughout his life.

He died recently, and although our relationship was strained, my husband and I cared for him until his death. He died peacefully, and I'm happy for him because since my mother passed 31 years ago, he has been ready to die every day. This world was not his home anymore.

Mama kept our home as normal as possible, and when we were young, Mama made sure that we were seen and not heard when he was home. That was a common way that children were raised back then.

Our parents loved us, but they never told us that. They didn't hug us. They provided for us, and we just knew that they loved us, but we didn't have a show of affection in our home. I didn't know that was important because I didn't have it growing up.

We received food, shelter, clothing, and discipline. We were not abused per se but cared for like a houseplant, more or less.

I didn't realize the effect that this had on me. In fact, I thought it was normal until I began to realize in my spirit that it wasn't, but I had no idea what to do about it either.

Sadly, I didn't raise my sons with that type of affection either.

I hope they know I love them with all of my heart, but I didn't know how to show it to them.

I didn't even know that I was supposed to show them.

I met their physical and material needs. I didn't mistreat them in any way. I was certainly not abusive to them, but I was neglectful because I didn't give them everything that they needed from me as a mother; they were my little houseplants too.

I just didn't know that as a family we were supposed to hug each other and say, I love you.

I know that sounds crazy, and looking back, it is crazy. How can a person not know to show affection? How is that not instinctive?

I know that we have a desire for affection in our spirit, soul, and body, but if it's not expressed, it will get suppressed. Mine got extremely suppressed. I regret it so much! My life and my family's life would have turned out so differently because I realize now how important love and affection are.

We did have happy times, but there was always something missing.

Our children were provided for very well except for the thing they needed the most.

I have learned this and take this advice. Let your children know how much you love them. Hug them and tell them that you love them every day, multiple times a day. You cannot do it too often or too much!

I didn't know what our family was missing until my sons grew up and married.

Then God sent two angels into our lives!

Their wives, our beautiful daughters-in-law (love), have brought something new into our world.

Showing love and affection by hugging us every time that they see us and saying, I love you.

It was not easy at first, but it was nice!

After many years of expressing love, our hearts have healed.

It's not awkward or uncomfortable anymore. We naturally greet them with a hug when they arrive and when they leave. In fact, I get as many hugs as I can because I need them; my hug bucket was pretty low! Lol

It's been a miraculous change, and it's made our life awesome and complete. I feel love, and I am capable of showing love now.

God is Good
All-Ways and Always!

I spent years feeling unlovable. If you don't show love to your children, they will grow up with guilt and shame. They will not have confidence. They will have low self-esteem. They will not even know why, but those feelings will be there.

I have regrets for not being able to show my sons and my husband how much I love them. We are still alive, and there is still time, so I am trying to make it up to them before I leave this world.

Thank God for this opportunity. Thank God for our angels that showed us the way!

***

Going back to my young life, I met all of the usual milestones that people meet. I went through school, learned to drive, and got a job. I wasn't happy in school.

I wasn't able to do things that others were doing. I had a few friends, but they were like me; we were never accepted into the big clique.

We were different partly because we wouldn't do the party scene. I believe mainly because we were poor and considered a lower class of people. Maybe I shouldn't say that; that sounds like Satan's lies!

Don't let anyone make you feel inferior to them because of your clothes, shoes, or house. You are loved by God and as important to him as anyone else. God created you the way that you are, and you are special.

It took me years to accept myself and to just be ok with myself, but now I know that God loves me. He thinks I am awesome; he wants to spend time with me. He's my father, so I am a daughter to a king!

***

Looking back, though, It could have also been that people sensed the lack of love and affection in my life. Maybe it was obvious, and I didn't realize it. I wasn't even aware of what I didn't have at that point.

I lived with a lot of guilt and shame. It had to be related to what I was missing in myself.

Satan robbed me in my youth, but God has put the pieces back together, and I'm living a purpose-filled life. Thank you, Jesus!

So being miserable at school, I dropped out in the 11th grade and got my GED because I had no chance of going to college at that point.

I was going straight to work; in fact, I was already working almost a full schedule. So, I decided that I could work more if I didn't go to school.

God is Good
All-Ways and Always!

***

I had dreams of being a nurse growing up. That was my chosen profession, but there was no money for me to go to college at that point in my life.

My parents worked hard, but paying the rent, with all of the other bills and buying food, took everything that they made.

I would follow in their footsteps. I couldn't imagine anything else because everyone that I was close to lived the same way. In fact, my dad told me on more than one occasion that I would not amount to anything else.

I can't be angry at him, though, because he was only speaking from his own experience. He came from an extremely poor family in the foothills of Tennessee. Any dreams that he had were squashed early in his life, and he didn't ever recover from that mindset. He raised us to think we were the underdogs and that we didn't have much of a chance in this life.

I went into adulthood with very skewed thinking. I didn't see the big picture of anything in my life. I lived in survival mode daily because that's how I saw my parents live.

They were doing the best that they could. I don't blame them; they raised me exactly like they were raised.

My dad was a hillbilly from a very small town in Tennessee. His dad was a tobacco farmer and a moonshiner.

Times were extremely hard, and they couldn't see any way out of their poverty-filled life on the mountain.

My dad's dad was murdered when he was around 12 years old. He and his brother had gone fishing and never returned. His uncle's body was found in the river, but his dad's (my grandfather's) body was never found.

For years everyone thought it was an accident.

My dad actually thought that his dad had murdered his uncle and had just left the family, thinking he was tired of taking care of them.

His dad was a mean man and was capable of doing that.

My dad used to search the phone book everywhere that we went for his dad's name. He hoped he would find him alive somewhere.

No doubt that if he had found him, he would have beaten him to a bloody pulp for leaving them.

The truth came out years later. An old man on his deathbed confessed to murdering my dad's dad and uncle.

The confession came too late!

Years of damage had been done to this family.

Because his dad's body was never found, his mom couldn't draw social security for the 6 children that she still had to raise on her own.

My dad said that they would have starved to death had it not been for other family members and the community.

A life that was hard just got harder. My grandmother always had a strained look on her face and a sadness in her eyes. She was sweet and kind, but I knew she was deeply wounded.

My dad left Tennessee at a very young age. He said he knew if he left that his mom would have one less mouth to feed.

He was only 16 when he ventured to Florida.

He landed a job at a local truck stop on Highway 19. That was a busy highway at the time.

That is where it all began. My mom's dad worked at that truck stop, as well as my granny, who cooked there, and a couple of aunts who waited tables.

My mom came from a family of 9 children.

My mom's parents had married when my granny was very young. People did that back then.

Marrying young was for economical reasons a lot of times. Families couldn't afford to feed all of the children that they had, so the teenagers would marry to reduce the stress on the family.

I'm not saying that was the reason that they married. I'm sure that they loved each other immensely.

After they got married, she didn't get pregnant for 7 years. She said that she thought that she couldn't have children at that point. When she finally did start having babies, she went on to have 9!

I only have two memories of my papa; that's what we called him. He died when I was just 4 years old, but I can see him vividly two times in my mind.

I really wished that I had gotten to know him; they say he was a good man.

My granny, I knew very well! She was something! A very special lady to me. I spent a lot of time with her growing up, and I loved her deeply.

She raised 9 children, one of whom was my mom, the middle child. My mom was awesome, sweet, kind, and always smiling.

To know her was to love her!

My granny was a businesswoman, owning and operating her own restaurant for many years from the 1960s to the 1970s.

She was a barrel of fun and laughs but a no-nonsense kind of woman! It wouldn't pay you to cross her.

She would do anything to help you, but don't try to help yourself at her expense.

She wore strength like a mink coat. She was elegant and classy.

Her hair never turned grey, and she told me that it never would as long as they had hair dye! lol I have so many fond memories of her and great times that we shared.

That's the kind of stock that my mom came from. Good, hardworking people. Who knew how to laugh and have fun?

My mom and dad met at that truck stop, and in time they married. My dad was a trucker and a diesel mechanic all of his life. He said if you own a semi-truck, you better know how to fix it because breakdowns on his old trucks were a definite thing.

I've seen him drive all day and work half of the night to repair his truck just so he could haul a load the next day.

My brother would be under that truck with him as much as possible, and he loved it. He would be covered with grease from head to toe.

Mechanical work suited my brother because he had to know how things worked.

He took everything apart as a kid and put it back together. Because he wanted to know what was inside of it and what made it operate.

I bet you can't guess what he's doing today and what he has done for over 40 years. Yep, diesel mechanic. He's not just any diesel mechanic either; I call him the diesel doctor.

He's highly trained and extremely knowledgeable in this field. On top of that, he loves it.

My dad was a trucker/mechanic, and my mom was a waitress most of her life. So, when I was growing up, I could see the writing on the wall.

God is Good
All-Ways and Always!

I knew that my future would consist of marriage, children, and work.

I looked forward to all three.

I wanted to be married, I wanted children, and I enjoy working. I've been officially working since I was 12 years old. My first job was a dishwasher in my granny's restaurant.

It was a busy bus stop and restaurant that stayed open 24 hours a day. I rode the school bus there after school and worked until 11pm.

I was paid $30 a week for 6 days of work. Do the math. That's not a lot of money, but I was glad to get it.

In my mind I was rich. I was just happy making my own money.

I wouldn't trade that experience because I learned a lot about dealing with the public and people in general.

If you want to have a good understanding of people, go to work in a restaurant. Although most people are so nice and pleasant. There are a few bad apples that stand out, and you will never forget those experiences. I don't remember their faces and didn't even know their names, but I remember the trouble that they caused.

There was always excitement there. I saw more than a few fights because all sorts of characters ride the bus.

They're not always happy people and definitely not always good.

You know Some people just go through life looking to cause trouble. It's not hard to recognize them and who they serve! They do the work of the devil wherever they go.

When you realize the spiritual authority that you have, though. People like that are easily dealt with. You do not have to stoop to their level to deal with them. It's really not that person giving you a hard time; it's a bad spirit on them. You can learn to rebuke that spirit in them and walk away the victor. If you try to diffuse them without using your spiritual authority, they just get worse.

I have encountered people who I know have a bad spirit in them who recognized Jesus in me. I've seen their faces almost contort when I smile at them.

They want to quickly get away from me because I will speak to them in the name of Jesus and rebuke them. I do it out loud but just under my breath so that I don't scare everyone around me. lol! If you use your spiritual authority, it works every time!

God commands us to love all people; you don't love their sin, but you must love them.

I have learned that how you treat people matters a lot! Keep that in mind when you are dealing with people. If they have a bad attitude, they may have a reason. You never know what a person is going through. It doesn't excuse them for being jerks, but if you knew the whole story. You might have more compassion for them.

When I encounter someone like that, I wonder what has happened to them.

I quickly say a prayer to rebuke Satan in their life and for God to bless them.

People are not the problem; it's the devil acting through them that is the problem. I try to remember that when dealing with people who are rude and annoying. It has changed the way that I deal with them and the outcome of our encounters on many occasions.

I am not perfect and never will be. I carried years of baggage around with me until Jesus Christ came into my heart to live. A weight has been lifted off of my shoulders, and the scales have been removed from my eyes, and I can see clearly now. That's what a relationship with Jesus will do for you.

I am sharing with you what I have learned from God's word. It's the key to success in this life.

***

I did eventually go to college and became an RN, my dream job. Being a nurse meant that I could help people when they needed it the most. Sick people need medical care, but most of all they need compassion.

Healing comes from God, but doctors and nurses are vessels to provide what God wants people to receive. God wants you well.

I was more than happy to show people that I cared through nursing. I gave them the best medical care that I could, but I also treated them with dignity and respect. I tried to meet their needs to the best of my ability.

No matter what job you do, you are working for God. Remember that when you go to work.

Your performance can honor God, or you can take advantage of your employer and goof off.

God is Good
All-Ways and Always!

Your employer may never know the time that you wasted on the clock when you were supposed to be working. Playing on your cell, hiding in the back corner of the storeroom, taking 20-minute bathroom breaks, etc. You may get away with it, and your employer may be none the wiser because they trust you.

God sees all of it, though. There isn't anything in life that he's not aware of.

God will bless you for always doing the right thing, especially when no one else is watching. God will bless you for working as if you are working for him. Your employer may not give you recognition or a raise, but God will bless you in ways that prosper you more than your employer ever could.

So don't just do enough to get by on your job. Go the extra mile. God is your provider and your source. If you want to be blessed abundantly, always do the next right thing. That's true in every area of your life. Keep doing what is right.

When faced with a decision to help someone in need. Don't judge people and withhold from them because you have the power to do so or because you think they don't deserve it. We are not supposed to judge people. You do what's right in God's eyes. They will be blessed, but you will be blessed even more.

When I hear of a need, I take that information as coming from God because if he got it to me, he must want me to do something about it. I have my spiritual eyes and ears open all the time. I'm ready to act when God reveals people in need. I do not want to miss an opportunity to do something for the Lord!

No matter what role that I have served in, I wanted to help people. Throughout my life, my peace and happiness came from doing for others. Whether it was for my immediate family, extended family, or strangers.

I am still like that. I am a server, and I am happy to be one. I go through life looking for ways to help others.

It may just be listening to them and giving them godly advice.

I am happy to do that too.

The best advice for anyone is to direct them to Jesus. He has provided everything that we need.

I am now a restaurant owner, and that's just another ministry to serve others through.

It provides the perfect atmosphere to show others that you care, but most importantly, that Jesus cares.

They say to keep religion and politics out of your business.

I never push my beliefs or views on people, but when the door opens up. I am not bashful to share them. It's for the sole purpose of bringing people to Jesus. He is worthy to be praised!

The restaurant business is in my blood. My grandmother had several restaurants as I was growing up, as well as aunts and uncles who did also.

I literally cut my teeth in a playpen in the kitchen while my mother worked the front of the house. The cook filled the orders and kept an eye on me. No doubt I was on her hip for part of the day as she prepared some of the best food you could put into your mouth. There isn't a better cook anywhere, hands down, than an old Southern cook.

My granny, who started the restaurant, was one of the best cooks I have ever known. I will add that my mother-in-law was as well.

Either one of them could take a few ingredients and make a feast fit for a king. No doubt they are cooking for one in heaven now.

It was a passion for them, and they loved to please people with good food. So I'm sure that's something they are still doing.

***

I grew up and married; the first marriage didn't work out. I was very young and very unprepared. I married 2 days after turning 17, and I had no idea what I was getting into. I just wanted to find what was missing in my life.

I was living with all of the baggage from childhood, and I was trying to escape it.

I didn't really know what I was missing until much later in life. Like I said, I lived each day in survival mode.

I will not bash my first husband; he was not prepared for marriage either, and he was doing the best that he could with what he knew at the time.

The divorce 4 years later was bitter and nasty, but I won't go into any of that because he is the father of my oldest son, and my son is a blessing.

I have never bashed his dad to him and never will.

Eventually, years after our divorce, my first husband apologized to me and asked for forgiveness for the way he had treated me.

I had forgiven him many years prior to that because if you don't forgive others, our father will not forgive us.

Matthew 6:15; KJV

"But if you forgive not men their trespasses, neither will your father forgive your trespasses.

I then met my husband of 40 years. He is my rock. He is the love of my life. When he was younger, he reminded me of Tom Selleck but more handsome. I can't imagine life without him.

He's a genius too! He can do anything and build anything.

One of our employees said that if he had been on the Titanic, there is no way that ship would have sunk—he would have engineered something to stop the leak! Lol!

He has that ability to fix things that aren't fixable and with limited resources.

He has two brothers that are the same way. I guess when you are raised poor and you can't just go buy what you need, you learn to adapt and overcome with what you have. That's my husband; he's an overcomer! He's really an awesome guy!

He has always provided well for our family. He has built amazing homes for us and our children from the ground up with his own hands. He's the Mr. Fix-It of the business, and I wouldn't want to do it without him.

He has put up with a lot from me because I was a very flawed person when we married. I knew what I wanted, but I didn't know how to get it. I didn't know how to do this love thing because of the lack of affection in my life growing up.

We both expressed love for each other in the beginning, but because I felt so unlovable. I doubted his love for me. I had severe low self-esteem, and I was so insecure. I couldn't believe that he loved me like he said he did. I was so afraid of losing his love because it scared me. I became obsessed with him and very jealous. My jealousy and insecurity actually pushed him away.

We are still together, but I did a lot of damage to our relationship. I love him very much, as well as all of my family.

There isn't a mean bone in my body. I just didn't understand love and didn't know how to accept it. I knew how to please people and take care of people, but I didn't know how to show love.

God is Good
All-Ways and Always!

The only reason our marriage has made it this long is because my husband didn't require affection either. He grew up in the same type of family that I did, except his parents were much stricter than mine.

So, we had a lot in common, we liked a lot of the same things, we both worked very hard, and we didn't argue.

We might disagree on things, but it doesn't turn into fights.

We have learned to give, accept, and forgive. That's the love that we have for each other.

Since I am telling you the story of my life, I will have to share a lot of truths about myself so that my story makes sense.

I always felt different. I knew something was missing. There had to be more to life than this.

I looked and acted completely normal, but on the inside there was a huge void.

I learned to be happy no matter what circumstances I was living in. That could have only come from God. I didn't even realize it at the time, but God was with me, giving me strength and encouragement.

Isaiah 41:10 says, "Fear thou not, for I am with thee; be not dismayed, for I am thy God; I will strengthen thee; yea, I will help thee; yea, I will uphold thee with the right hand of my righteousness."

God is with you always. You may not be acknowledging God or serving him, but he never leaves you. It took years for me to realize that, but now I know that he is always with me and you. He's not just my God; he is yours too if you believe.

***

I have so much to tell you, and I pray that I don't miss making a point. I want it to click with you like it clicked within me. I pray for the Holy Spirit's guidance because I have had some real revelations in life, and all of them came from studying God's word, the Bible. It has changed my life. I want to share them with you because I know it will change your life too.

Where do I begin? I will begin with a prayer for you and me.

Heavenly Father, in Jesus' name, I pray that you give me the words to write that you want to speak to anyone who reads this book.

We are your vessels here on earth, and we are here to spread the good news about you and your son, our savior Jesus.

God is Good
All-Ways and Always!

Let your words flow freely through me to reach lost souls and saved ones who are struggling in this life.

You have provided us with everything that we need to succeed in life and to have a wonderful life here on earth.

I know that you did not intend for us to live in misery and grief.

I also know that it's our choice to live in victory or to live defeated.

I thank you for helping me write this book to teach people what you have taught me through so many wonderful ministers, pastors, teachers, evangelists, and apostles, but most importantly through your word, the Holy Bible.

I pray that whoever reads this book receives the message that you want them to receive.

We give you honor, glory, and praise always, in Jesus' name! Amen!

I have learned that the Bible is not just a book; it's a guide to live by. It should be required reading in schools and colleges. It's the most important book that you will ever read because when you read it, it reads you.

It will guide you to make the best decisions based on what God wants for you and what Jesus paid for you to have.

You see, as a Christian, you are entitled to things to help you live a better life here on earth. Jesus provided them for you through his death, burial, and resurrection.

He defeated sin, sickness, poverty, and so much more.

You were not born to just get by in life; you are NOT supposed to live in sickness, poverty, or misery. Your life doesn't have to be falling apart all of the time; you have a choice.

Accepting Jesus as your savior has so many more benefits than assuring you will go to heaven when you die.

You receive power to live an awesome, abundant life here on earth. You have authority over Satan's attacks, but you have to cooperate through faith to use that power in your life.

It's not something that you can earn by being good. It's a gift that you receive when you accept Jesus as your savior.

You do have to know how to use it to move things from the spiritual realm into the physical realm, and that is through faith.

When we ask God for something, he answers yes, but because he's a spirit, the answer is in the spiritual realm.

God doesn't live in our physical world. He works through us spiritually to produce things physically. That's why if you are praying for a financial miracle, it comes from someone here on earth; money just doesn't fall from the sky! You pray and ask God for what you need, you believe that you receive through faith, and it happens.

You are a spirit, you have a soul (mind, will, and emotions), and you have a body.

When you accept Jesus as your savior, through faith, your spirit is made completely righteous that instant; you are morally right. Jesus paid for all of your sins—past, present, and future. At that moment in God's eyes, you are as pure as Jesus, completely sinless. It's as if you have never sinned in your life. He remembers your sin no more. That's why when you accept Jesus as your savior. You can let go of your guilt and shame. You instantly became a child of God!

You do have a part in your salvation. You have to believe it to receive it. It just takes faith!

We are going to talk a lot about faith throughout this book. It's so important and so easy once you decide to trust God for whatever you need.

No matter what the situation is or how big the problem is.

Nothing is impossible with God! Nothing is too big, and I mean nothing!

"But Jesus beheld them and said unto them, with men this is impossible, but with God all things are possible." Matthew 19:26; KJV.

I'll tell you how simple it is. When you go to sit down in a chair, do you believe that it will hold your weight when you sit? Think about it. You trust that chair, and you don't doubt that it will hold your weight, or you would never sit in it. You don't give it a second thought. You see the chair, and you just sit.

You know without a doubt that it will support you. You sit down, and the chair supports you. You don't fall. You don't get hurt. You just sit.

That's what it takes to trust God. You just have to do it.

God is Good
All-Ways and Always!

That is faith in a nutshell!

Don't think about it; just do it.

If you can believe a chair will hold your weight. You can believe that God loves you and Jesus loves you and he paid the price for your sins. You can trust that God only wants what is best for you because it's true and it's promised in the Bible. God's spoken words on paper in black and white.

Proverbs 3:5-6; KJV says, "Trust in the Lord with all your heart; do not lean on your own understanding. In all of your ways acknowledge him, and he shall direct your paths ".

Those are a couple of my favorite verses in the Bible. We are supposed to rely on God's word for wisdom and supernatural understanding, not our own human understanding. We were not created to operate without God's guidance. We were given free will to do so, but when we stop depending on God, we create destruction in our lives.

We cannot live up to our God-given potential without God being active in our lives. Reaching the ultimate life requires a relationship with God and faith.

***

Have you ever wished that you had a guidebook for your life? That you could follow and go step by step. Chapter by chapter, and know exactly what you need to do so that you don't mess things up?

I have always said that I wish that I would have had a book like that. Well, little did I know that it was available. I missed it for 50 years. I didn't know that if I had been reading the Bible all of my life. Although it didn't say my name specifically and tell me to do this or to do that.

I would have been led by the powerful Holy Spirit to make better decisions that would allow God to bless me more.

It would've kept me out of a lot of trouble and situations that I regretted being in, and it would've prevented a lot of heartache.

I never really sought God in decisions throughout my life. Mainly because I didn't know that he wanted to help me. I really felt like I had to do the best I could and make decisions on my own.

I didn't know how much God loves me and how much he loves all of us. I didn't know that he had written the Bible to guide us. I thought it was just full of stories about his life. I was so wrong, and I can't stress enough to read the Bible.

God is Good
All-Ways and Always!

If you don't understand every part of it, it's ok. The Holy Spirit will make sure that you understand what you need to. The more that you read and study, the more that you'll understand it.

I promise if you open the Bible and read it, your focus in life will shift. It may be subtle at first, but you will see that you become more positive and happier. Things will change for you.

You will develop a sense of well-being that can't be explained other than it's a peace and comfort that only comes from having a relationship with Jesus. If you seek God, you will find him, and he will bless you immensely.

I know it sounds like it will be a drag! I used to think that too. What could be gained by reading some dusty old book about a man who lived over 2000 years ago?

That's exactly why I wrote this book. There is so much to gain I can't even list it all! There is so much more to lose if you don't read it and follow God's guidance.

You have a chance to change your life. You have everything that you need to live a life you've only dreamed of.

I'm going to share how my life changed, and I pray that it gives you hope for your life too.

All glory to God and our savior Jesus Christ for my life and for inspiring me to write this book to bless you.

***

What you focus on, you become.

Proverbs 23:7, KJV, says, "For as a man thinketh in his heart, so is he."

You have to think about a sin before you do it. It's usually subtle at first. You will feel convicted at the first thought too; in your spirit you know that it's wrong.

It doesn't matter if you're saved or not; God instilled a conscience into everyone, and we all know when we are sinning.

If you don't stop sin at the first thought, through prayer and God's word.

The desire to sin grows, and your thoughts become actions.

It's not a sin to have the thought as long as you don't dwell on it or actually follow through to do it.

God is Good
All-Ways and Always!

We all have thoughts that come into our heads, and Satan is the source of the bad ones!!

Don't let him get a foothold into your life through your thoughts. Stop them before they grow because they will progress if you let them; the devil will make sure of that.

The battle is won in your mind, but you can't win without Jesus.

Submit your thoughts to Jesus. You have to empower yourself by reading God's word and talking to him.

You can talk to him just like you do anyone else. There isn't a formal prayer or ritual to follow.

He just wants a relationship with you.

It matters what you fill your head with. I know you have heard the phrase garbage in and garbage out.

You can spend time filling your mind with anything.

You can fill it with good things like God's word and promises, or you can fill it with worldly things.

The world offers everything imaginable to expose you to evil.

With the invention of smartphones, we have it in the palm of our hand. You can google anything. You can google the vilest things imaginable, and they pop up on the screen.

It can also be used to read the Bible and watch the greatest preachers too.

Be careful what entertains you!

If it's not good, the devil will be right there in your mind, working all of it against you. You may think that it's just entertainment, but it's not! That's exactly what Satan wants you to think.

He will tell you that this has no impact on your life, but that's a lie from the pits of hell!

No surprise because Satan is the father of all lies; he first deceives you, and then he can control you!

When we let evil things into our minds. Satan uses it as a portal to enter into our lives and cause all kinds of havoc! Yes, that's how it works!

I used to read my horoscope daily. That sounds innocent enough, right? I thought it was entertaining. I was surprised when some of my days actually turned out the way that my horoscope had predicted. Who doesn't want to know what our future holds?

I began to be dependent on that reading. I didn't know at that time that Satan is the designer of the horoscope and other fortune-telling sources. They are forms of sorcery and witchcraft.

God doesn't use a horoscope because he wants us to have faith and trust in him for each day.

He provided his word to predict our future. All of the guidance that we need is written in the Bible.

Satan cannot do anything to you that you don't give him permission to do.

He will entice you with sin and make it so desirable that you won't resist it unless your faith and trust in Jesus are strong.

Through Jesus we have everything that we need to resist the devil and live victoriously.

You don't have to bow to Satan. Don't let him control your life.

Jesus provided everything that you need to defeat him.

It does take effort on your part. You only have to accept and cooperate through faith; you only have to believe.

In the Bible in Mark 9:23, KJV, Jesus said unto him, If thou canst believe, all things are possible to him that believeth.

The way I read that is as plain and simple as you can get. All things are possible if you believe!

That's a powerful verse that gives you hope.

No matter what situation you are in or battles that you face. There is a prevention or resolution spelled out in the book of love written by God our Father.

Don't let Satan start telling you that God's word won't work for you. Don't let him say that you are unworthy or can't be forgiven.

That's Satan's playbook 101!

Jesus came, especially for you, no matter who you are or what you have done.

People do not realize the power that is in the Bible, or everyone would be walking around reading it instead of having their heads buried in a cell phone all the time.

If you don't read your Bible, you are powerless against the attacks of Satan.

He knows God's word from cover to cover. He knows that if you read it to renew your mind, he has no power over you.

He knows that you will realize the power that you have been given through salvation. We are heir to everything that Jesus is heir to, and we have been given spiritual authority to defeat the devil and his attacks.

I'm not a saint either, so I'm not coming down on you, but I have realized how important it is to study the Bible and to truly do what it says.

Put your faith and trust in God because when you do, things change in your life. You will have peace in the storms of your life. God will bless you and provide for you, and you will be healthy, prosperous, happy, and at peace.

Hey, you can take my advice or leave it, but I'm speaking from experience.

I've messed things up before, and I wished I had known that there was true guidance, true help, and true peace.

If I had trusted God, it would have kept me out of a lot of trouble and prevented a lot of headaches and heartaches for me and the people that I love.

Satan doesn't want you to know the truth.

He likes it when you live defeated, sick, miserable, poor, and in fear.

If you go through life and you never realize what you have inside of you, then he wins.

You have power and authority over Satan and all of his demons.

If you focus on your problem more than God, you let Satan dominate you and rob you of everything that God wants you to have.

You have to change that. You have been given spiritual authority through Jesus.

You have the same power that raised Jesus from the dead living inside of you.

That should make you feel different! That should give you hope.

You can rest knowing that Jesus took care of everything. You just have to believe (have faith) to reap the benefits.

There is more to Jesus' work on the cross than forgiveness of sins.

With accepting Jesus as our savior, we are not only assured that we are going to heaven to live forever when we leave this earth, but we also become a new person in our spirit.

God is Good
All-Ways and Always!

You don't need anything else ever, spiritually. Your spirit is complete. You have all of the faith, joy, and power that God will ever give you.

Jesus provided for our healing so that we are restored from sickness or injury here on earth.

He provided for our prosperity so that we can live in a state of financial success.

He provided for our righteousness because we have been made morally right through him; we are free from guilt and shame.

He provided for our justification because we moved from a state of sin to grace and under grace. Salvation is a free gift from God through Jesus. We cannot earn it; we just have to accept it by faith.

He provided forgiveness because our sin is no longer held against us; our slates have been wiped clean.

We have been sanctified, purified if you will, because all of our sins are removed and forgotten, and God remembers them no more.

We have been glorified to complete our salvation to the full realization of what Jesus did for us.

2 Corinthians 5:17, KJV, says, "Therefore if any man be in Christ, he is a new creature; old things are passed away; behold, all things are become new."

God is good all ways and always! His promises are always true; he is faithful to fulfill them in our lives if we trust him. God will never let you down!

The easiest way to live and receive all of the blessings that God has planned for you is to seek him above everything else.

Spend time reading his words and talking to him through prayer or just conversation.

I just talk to him throughout the day the same way that I would talk to you.

The Bible says to pray without ceasing, so I stay in a constant state of prayer.

That way, when the enemy starts trying to attack; I'm ready to win because just by speaking the name of Jesus in faith, it will send him packing!

You have to read your Bible to stand against his attacks, though. We can't do anything on our own without faith, the word, the Holy Spirit, and Jesus.

God has provided everything that we need to succeed in his word. It instructs us about everything that we will have to deal with in our lives.

There isn't a subject that isn't covered in the Bible.

God is Good
All-Ways and Always!

It doesn't do any good to read it if you don't plan on using it.

If you put God first in your life, truly seek him and trust him. You will be amazed at how God will work in your life.

It says in Matthew 6:33 "But seek ye first the kingdom of God and his righteousness, and all of these things will be added unto you. "

When you decide to put your faith and trust in God. You can actually rest. You can relax knowing that he has taken care of everything. You can let go of worry because he's promised to never leave us or forsake us.

Do not worry because worry isn't faith; it's unbelief.

Unbelief will stop your prayers from being answered and will stop God's blessings in your life.

In Matthew 7:7, the Bible says, "Ask, and it shall be given you; seek, and ye shall find; knock, and it shall be opened unto you."

Matthew 7:8, "For everyone that asketh receiveth; and he that seeketh findeth; and to him that knocketh it shall be opened."

Nowhere in that verse does it say maybe or not you. It says everyone who asks receives, if you seek, you find, and if you knock, it shall be opened.

God isn't hiding from you!

In other words, if you seek God with your whole heart, you will find him. He is waiting on you to reach out to him by faith. He's waiting to answer your prayers and give you whatever you have faith to receive.

God will meet you where your faith is.

***

Faith is really simple; human faith only believes what we can experience with our 5 senses. Seeing, hearing, smelling, tasting, and feeling.

It's easy to believe when you already see what you are asking for, right?

If you ask me for a new car and I tell you that I am going to give you a new car and you see it in front of you.

You hear me say that it's yours; take the keys and drive away. That didn't take much faith.

You could see it before you received it.

That is not the faith that God is looking for.

We have to have God faith, where we believe without seeing, a childlike faith. Children believe us when we tell them things.

They just take our word for it because they know that we will provide for them. We will do what we say we will do.

When we trust God, we need to be like a child and just believe because God's word promises us that he will answer our prayers.

Your earthly father wants you to have things, the best that he can provide. How much more does your Heavenly Father want you to have things?

His word says that by Jesus' stripes we were healed. If you are sick and you want to be healed, don't let go of that promise.

His word says he is with us always, and he will never leave us nor forsake us. If you are going through a rough time, don't let go of that promise.

There are so many more promises. His words are true, and he will never fail us.

I know you are probably saying, Easier said than done. I understand that. There was a time that I didn't know how to use my faith too.

I didn't even know I was supposed to have faith.

That's why I'm writing this book. I can tell you that faith works, and it works every time.

It's a little scary letting go and letting God. If you have never put your complete trust in God for an answer to your problems, then you're not sure if your faith will work.

It will work if you believe it will work. That's what makes it work. Your belief makes it work. Faith is believing without seeing the outcome.

God will never fail you. He loves you too much, and he's made these promises to you, and he will always come through for you.

***

What I have learned on my journey is that I can change anything in my life.

I cannot do anything in my own power but through Jesus. I can do anything.

Philippians 4:13; KJV. says, "I can do all things through Christ, which strengtheneth me."

Your life is going to be consumed by good or evil. You either go all in for Jesus or you go all in with the devil.

Jesus doesn't want you to be a halfway Christian. You cannot straddle the fence. God cannot and will not bless you if you are lukewarm for him. If you don't use your faith, your life will not change. You will continue to struggle because you are no match against the devil without Jesus!

The only way that we don't get what we believe God is for is because we failed God.

We lost faith, or we let our faith waver. We gave up before the thing that we were believing God for manifested; that's not true faith.

The faith that God expects doesn't give up, doesn't doubt, but holds steady until the blessings come!

God never fails us! Faith in God works, and it works every time. God is always faithful, and his answer is always yes and amen.

When we pray and ask God for something. He answers immediately, Yes and amen!

I know you're thinking that's not how it works for me.

You probably do not see the answer right away, but God answered right away, and he said yes.

So why didn't your problem change immediately? It's because God is in the spiritual realm. We are in the physical or natural realm.

We have a spirit that communicates with God in the spiritual realm, but we don't live with him yet.

So, the answer comes from God, but we have to move it from the spiritual world into our natural world.

That takes faith, which you already have. We have been given all of the faith that we will ever need when we get saved.

***

There isn't a special ritual that you have to do to receive; you just have to believe it. Speak it out of your mouth and don't doubt it.

I wrote this book to get a message out to everyone as quickly as possible. The message of faith is simple, but most people either don't know about it or they don't believe it! If you don't believe that faith works, it won't!

Faith is a law that God created; the message of faith is covered throughout the Bible. Faith is important to God; in fact, without faith it is impossible to please God.

Hebrews 11:6, KJV, says, "But without faith it is impossible to please him: for he that cometh to God must believe that he is and that he is a rewarder of them that diligently seek him."

You cannot just believe that God can do something in your situation; you must believe that he will do it.

If you don't believe that he will do it, then you are in unbelief. God cannot bless you if you don't believe.

It's not that he doesn't want to, but you have a part in receiving from him, and that is believing with all of your heart.

***

You may be thinking that God will answer prayers for other people but not for you.

There is no one more deserving than you.

I'm going to tell you something that may surprise you, but God loves you!

God only has love for you because he is love.

God wants to bless you, and he wants you to have an abundant life here on earth, not just when you get to heaven.

Don't ever let anyone tell you that God is mad at you or that he will stop loving you because that is a lie straight from the lips of Satan!!

God isn't capable of not loving you. God knew you before you were born, and he had plans for you from the time you were conceived.

Jeremiah 29:11, KJV, says, "For I know the thoughts I have for you, saith the Lord, thoughts of peace and not of evil, to give you an expected end."

That defines love. God's plans are only good for you. When we follow his plan for our life, we are assured of an expected end. When we encounter evil in our lives, it's because we aren't following God's plan.

If you are wondering what God's plans are for your life here on earth,. Seek God because he is the one who created you; he's got the playbook for your life, and he will guide you every step of the way.

You may be thinking that if he planned my life, why does it suck?!

If your life sucks, it's because you have let Satan have the control and victory!

It's not God's fault! It's not his will for you! Oh, and it's not your parents' fault either!

You'll understand that by the time you finish this book, so stay with me and keep reading, because if your life is screwed up, it is fixable!

This book is about making right decisions for your life that will bring blessings from God. It's also about how to deal with the attacks from Satan on a daily basis.

God is Good
All-Ways and Always!

If you are trusting God and are actively pursuing a relationship with Jesus, Satan is attacking you! I know that from experience!

The closer that you get to God, the more Satan attacks. That's because Satan wants to rob you of the life that God wants you to have.

You have to be tenacious in trusting God through it all. Keep Jesus close by because he's the answer for everything. All of the strength that you will need comes from him; use it!

If you get angry when things are not going right. Don't take it out on your family. Turn that anger towards Satan and let him have it! Talk to him like the jerk that he is! You have that authority!

***

I was a product of wrong teaching. I was taught to fear not only my parents but God!

I was never taught that God was love or that he loves us.

I didn't understand love like I do now. My parents were strict, and I walked on eggshells a lot. I know they were trying to raise me with good manners and to be morally right to the best of their understanding and ability.

I believed that God was watching and ready to bring the hammer down on me anytime I sinned. I didn't understand that he loves us.

I viewed him as a tyrant, and my service to him was out of sheer fear.

You cannot serve God out of fear; you should honor him and have a healthy fear of him, but because you respect him. He is our creator, and he loves us.

We should serve him out of love because he first loved us. He gave us life, and he gave us Jesus. Who died to save us and set us free from the curse?

We are no longer victims without hope, but we are blessed children of God!

Heirs to salvation and the kingdom, joint heirs with Jesus.

That means that anything that Jesus has, we have it too!

I am an imperfect human. I've sinned a lot! So, I walked around with shame and guilt most of my life.

When bad things happened to me, I felt like I deserved it, and I was grateful that the "punishment" from God wasn't worse!

God is Good
All-Ways and Always!

It was a miserable life! I didn't understand that it wasn't God causing all of the bad things to happen to me, and it wasn't God punishing me either. I did not understand that all bad things come from the devil and only good things come from God.

I didn't understand that Jesus paid for our sins so that we don't have to be punished by God.

I was trying to please God on my own but was failing to realize that I couldn't be good enough to live up to his expectations.

I was neglecting to realize that Jesus had already paid the price for me and that I didn't have to—in fact, that I could never live good enough.

I was trying to live according to the Old Testament, following the Ten Commandments.

Under the old covenant, the only way to be right with God would be if you didn't break any of the commandments. That's impossible!

Jesus was the only sinless person on earth.

Thank God for Jesus! He came into the world and defeated Satan. We are no longer under the old covenant.

We are under the New Covenant; we have been given new rules to follow. Now the only thing that we have to do to please God is just accept Jesus as our savior, and we are saved. Then we have spiritual authority to defeat Satan in our lives!

God has a plan to save you and to bless you. He gave his son Jesus for you. God is good, and all good things come from him. God is good all ways and always!

Satan is vile, wicked, and evil, and every bad thing comes from him! If things are not going well in your life. Satan is the reason. He wants you to think it's God's judgment on you, but that is a lie.

If you are a Christian, Jesus paid the judgment for you. You could never atone for your own sins in God's eyes, but you don't have to because Jesus already did.

***

I used to think, what is our purpose? Is life just a game that God plays? I mean, he knows we're going to mess up, and is he just waiting there to take us down? No, he's not! I was wrong, and if you feel that way, this book is for you.

God is Good
All-Ways and Always!

What I am sharing with you I learned later in life. I want to tell you about it now so that you can apply these principles to your life.

You will understand that you have power through Jesus to fight Satan in every area of your life!

He has no authority over you, but he wants you to think he does.

If I had known how much God loves us and wants the absolute best for us.

If I had understood what it meant when Jesus sacrificed his life for us.

It would've changed my world a long time ago.

Jesus' death, burial, and resurrection meant that we were given spiritual authority over the enemy, Satan.

Luke9; KJV "Behold, I give unto you power to tread on serpents and scorpions, and over all of the power of the enemy: and nothing shall by any means harm you"

That verse is speaking about spiritual authority; it doesn't mean that Satan won't attack and that we will never experience any physical pain or any tribulation.

It does mean that when you come under his attack, the power in you through Jesus can defeat him.

I lost years to pain and suffering that wasn't necessary because I did not know what I had. I have learned to use my Jesus-given spiritual authority against Satan, and he cringes when I get up in the morning. Not because of me but because of Jesus' power in me and my ability to use it! Haha!

My life is so good now I will not look back but keep moving forward and thanking God for each new day because of the revelation that he has given me. I'm blessed beyond measure!

God intended for us to be blessed on earth, not just in heaven. If I had known the power that lives in us through Jesus' sacrifice and death.

I would've been able to stand against evil in my life and truly receive the blessings that God wants us to have long before now.

I know now! Satan be damned to hell! Your reign over me is gone! I refuse to let the enemy win. Jesus gave his life for us to be able to fight! I am doing my part.

My life is way different than it used to be. I'm sharing this with you because your life can change today.

CHAPTER 2

The first thing that you have to do is accept Jesus as your savior. Jesus came to save the world, but he came especially for you.

There is a very popular song that says when Jesus was on the cross, you were on his mind. That is the truth for Christians: he knows you by name.

He knows every part of your life, and he loves you regardless of your sins and failures.

If you have never accepted Jesus as your savior, take a moment to do so. It will be the most important decision that you will ever make.

Pray this prayer; speak it out of your mouth. Believe it in your heart, and you will be saved. Jesus died for your sins; he was buried and rose again on the third day to redeem us from the curse that the world came under after Adam and Eve sinned against God.

Dear Lord Jesus, I know I am a sinner. Please forgive me for my sins. I believe that you died for my sins. I believe that you were buried and rose again on the third day. I believe that you are alive today, making intercession for me to God, my father. Amen

If you prayed that prayer and you believed in your heart that those words are true, then you are saved!

The Bible says, "If thou shalt confess with thy mouth the Lord Jesus, and shalt believe in thine heart that God raised him from the dead, thou shalt be saved. For with the heart man believeth unto righteousness; and with the mouth confession is made unto salvation." Romans 10:9-10, KJV.

Notice that the scripture says that you have to believe in your heart—that's faith—and confess it with your mouth—that's works.

"For the body without the spirit is dead, so faith without works is dead also"—James 2:26, KJV.

The power of God just filled your body with his spirit. Your spirit is the same as God now. The same spirit that raised Jesus Christ from the dead.

You have now been given authority over the evil in your life.

God is Good
All-Ways and Always!

I know you may not be familiar with what I'm talking about.

My hope and my prayer is that you have faith to believe this.

I pray this clicks in your mind, spirit, soul, and body!

You just accepted Jesus as your savior through faith.

You believed in him and what he did for you, although you did not see him. You didn't witness him being tortured, beaten, dying, and rising again.

You just accepted it by faith, and that's exactly what you have to do to be saved.

CHAPTER 3

When I was growing up, I went to church often, pretty much every time the door was open from the age of 10.

I would listen to the preacher and often wonder if that was it. Is that all the Bible has to say?

I was raised in a Baptist church, and the main sermon was salvation.

While that is the most important message and the most important decision that you need to make in your life.

Do it before it's too late. If you die and you haven't accepted Jesus as your savior, you will be sent to hell to live for eternity.

You are going to live forever; after you die, you will either live forever in heaven or in hell.

God is Good
All-Ways and Always!

If you accept Jesus as your savior, believe he was beaten for your sickness. He died for your sins, he was buried and went to hell, and he was raised on the third day.

He defeated sickness, pain, poverty, suffering, sin, and death. So that we could live in health, peace, joy, happiness, and prosperity on earth.

He came so that we could have life and have it more abundantly. Here on earth, in this life. Then when we die, we will spend eternity with him in paradise.

If you do not accept Jesus as your savior, not only will you live a defeated life here on earth, but when you die, you will spend eternity in hell.

Jesus describes hell as a place of eternal torment, unquenchable fire. Where the worm does not die and where people will gnash their teeth in anguish and pain.

They will live this way forever and will be separated from God forever; it will be misery beyond what we can comprehend.

There's a story in the Bible of a rich man who knew a poor beggar who sat at his gate and begged for food. The rich man didn't feed him; he ignored him.

They both died, and the rich man went to hell, and the poor beggar went to heaven.

The rich man could look up from hell and see the beggar who had gone to heaven. He pleaded for the beggar to be able to wet his finger and come and touch his tongue because he was so thirsty.

This tells me those in hell will be able to see people in heaven and realize that they could be there too if they had accepted Jesus.

That will be unbearable torment in itself to see Jesus and loved ones in heaven and never be able to communicate with them again but realize that you could have chosen to accept Jesus as your savior and you would be there too! Accept Jesus before it's too late!

As I was saying, salvation is most important; however, I always felt like there had to be more to God's word besides salvation. The preachers that I heard never preached on anything else. I would often think, I'm saved. Now what?

I would read verses in the Bible about healing and miracles, but I was led to believe that those things went away when Jesus and the disciples went away.

God is Good
All-Ways and Always!

I was led to believe that sickness actually came from God!

I was taught that God didn't really like us and we had to beg for his love, and if you did something wrong, he was just waiting to make you suffer.

To make you sick, kill you, or make your life so miserable you wish you were dead. It was frightening!

CHAPTER 4

It wasn't until I was 50 years old that I really began to study the Bible. Up until then I listened to pastors and teachers, but I didn't really study or research on my own.

Since then, I've had a hunger for the word of God and a desire to know everything about him, his son Jesus, his word, and the mysteries of living this life we are living.

We only have this one life to live, so how you live matters a lot!

The idea that God is waiting to harm you or punish you is an absolute lie from Satan! When you are born again, saved, and accept Jesus as your savior, you are adopted by God.

You are a child of God from that point on.

God is your father at that point. Would your father make you sick? Would your father want to kill you? Or would your father want the absolute best for you?

God is Good
All-Ways and Always!

Of course, your father wants the absolute best for you. Your earthly father is limited in his ability to provide for you because he's living in a fallen world, but God owns the world, so he has an unlimited supply for you!

You will have to cooperate to receive, though, and that's what we are covering in this book.

God wants to bless you in all ways and always. Sometimes we make it impossible for him to do so.

We can separate ourselves from God by our own actions and the choices that we make.

If we choose to live in sin, we can hinder God's blessings for us because he cannot reward bad behavior.

That doesn't mean that God leaves you or stops loving you because he doesn't; he's incapable of doing that!

"Be strong and of good courage, fear not, nor be afraid of them: for the Lord thy God, he it is that doth go with thee; he will not fail thee, nor forsake thee."
—Deuteronomy 31:6, KJV

Our choices and actions can hinder God from being able to bless us, but you can repent and come back to him anytime. He forgives and forgets every time. He is always waiting for you to come back to him. He wants you to have the best life on earth because God is good all ways and always!

CHAPTER 5

Now I'm going to cover the most important part of living an awesome life here on earth.

You must be baptized in the Holy Ghost/Spirit. This is a separate act from salvation. It's not a requirement to go to heaven, but it is absolutely vital to living a successful Christian life here on earth. The Holy Ghost is a separate person. God is three people: the Father, the Son (or the word and the Holy Ghost.

We receive God's spirit at salvation, but to supercharge it, you have to ask God to baptize you in the Holy Ghost. He will do it when you ask for it, and if you believe that you receive it, it takes faith.

God wants us to receive the Holy Ghost because he knows that we need it, and he created him to be a comforter for us since he is not physically with us here on earth.

God is Good
All-Ways and Always!

Acts 19:2-4, KJV, says, "He said unto them, Have ye received the Holy Ghost since ye believed? And they said unto him, We have not so much as heard there be any Holy Ghost."

When Jesus was preparing to leave earth after his resurrection, he told the disciples that it was important that he go away because then the Holy Ghost would come to be with them always.

As a man, Jesus was limited and could not be with everyone or everywhere at the same time, but his spirit living in them after he left could be with everyone all the time, and that's true for us too.

John 16:7, KJV. "Nevertheless, I tell you the truth; it is expedient for you that I go away, for if I go not away, the comforter will not come unto you; but if I depart, I will send him unto you."

Jesus was even anointed with the Holy Ghost by God while he was on this earth. If Jesus needed to be anointed, how much more do we need him?

Acts 10:38, KJV: "How God anointed Jesus of Nazareth with the Holy Ghost and with power: who went about doing good and healing all that were oppressed of the devil: for God was with him."

Notice in that verse that the word says healing is good and the devil causes the oppression.

The devil is bad, and all bad things come from him. God is good all ways and always!

The Holy Spirit, or Holy Ghost, is the power source in our lives as believers. We have the same Holy Spirit that Jesus was anointed with, and we can do the same miraculous works that he did if we believe.

Mark 16:17-18, KJV. "And these signs shall follow them that believe: in my name they shall cast out devils; they shall speak with new tongues. They shall take up serpents; and if they drink any deadly thing, it shall not hurt them; they shall lay hands on the sick, and they shall recover."

That says that we will do every miracle that Jesus did. In fact, Jesus said we will do even greater works than him if we believe.

John 14:12; KJV. "Verily, verily, I say unto you. He that believeth on me, the works that I do shall he do also, and greater works than these shall he do; because I go to my father."

The Holy Spirit is sent to teach us all things and bring to our remembrance what Jesus has spoken to us, but he doesn't automatically work in our lives when we are saved. You must receive him by faith.

John 14:26; KJV. "But the comforter, which is the Holy Ghost, whom the Father will send in my name, he shall teach you all things and bring all things to your remembrance, whatsoever I have said unto you."

We must ask God to be filled with the Holy Spirit and believe that we receive, just like we did for salvation, and God fills you immediately. It's a gift; you don't have to earn it, you just have to ask, believe, and receive it.

When you are filled with the Holy Spirit, you will be able to speak in other tongues. Why do you want to do that? you ask.

It's because speaking in tongues is a prayer language between you and God. Your spirit speaks directly to him. Your mind is out of the way so you are not trying to come up with words to pray. Your spirit knows what to say to God, and he understands you.

The act of speaking in tongues edifies you and your spirit, and you become a powerhouse for God.

Acts 2:4, KJV. "And they were filled with the Holy Ghost and began to speak with other tongues, as the spirit gave them utterance."

How to speak in other tongues After you have asked God to fill you with the Holy Spirit, you just open your mouth and start speaking the sounds that come out of your mouth. This is your spiritual language with God.

If you want to know what you speak, you can pray and ask God for interpretation of God's mysteries revealed to you.

The way it works is you speak in tongues and believe God for interpretation, then revelation comes to you.

I speak in tongues all throughout the day. If it comes up in my spirit to speak it, I will, especially if there is some conflict going on around me.

It's my safe place to run to the Father and have that secret conversation with him.

Ephesians 3:20, KJV. "Now unto him that is able to do exceedingly abundantly above all that we ask or think, according to the power that worketh in us."

God can do anything through us that we allow him to do. He can only work if we have faith to believe, though, and have power working through us from the Holy Spirit.

God wants to give us revelation through the Holy Spirit. Through the Holy Spirit, we have access to God's wisdom.

God is Good
All-Ways and Always!

1 Corinthians 2:12-14; KJV. "Now we have received, not the spirit of the world but the spirit which is of God, that we might know the things that are freely given to us of God."

The most powerful thing that you are entitled to as a Christian is the Holy Spirit. When you accept Jesus as your savior, God's spirit comes to live on the inside of you. You have the power to fight Satan's attacks, but you need a helper. That is where the Holy Spirit comes in.

The Holy Spirit is powerful, but most believers do not realize the power that is available to them. Therefore, they do not live up to their God-given potential.

Just like it takes faith for forgiveness, salvation, healing, etc. It takes faith to ignite the Holy Spirit in you.

If you do not choose to receive the Holy Spirit, your life will not look any different than unbelievers. We live in the same fallen world and face the same struggles, but as a Christian, you have a promise of a better life if you choose to use the power tools that God gave us.

I am not saying that you won't go through attacks and difficulties. In fact, if you go all in for God and choose to live this power-filled life, Satan is going to try harder to take you down, but remember the Holy Spirit in you is stronger than him!

You can choose how Satan's attacks affect you. You can speak to your problems (mountains) to be removed with the spiritual authority that you have. You have God, Jesus, the Holy Spirit, and angels backing you up, and they are willing and available to come to your aid.

CHAPTER 6

The Bible is full of God's promises, but just because they're in the Bible doesn't mean they're going to automatically work for you. Why? Because you have a part in causing them to work.

You can read them all you want to. You can memorize every word, but that's not what makes them work. You have to believe them and SPEAK them out of your mouth, out loud.

The Bible says in Proverbs 18:21, KJV, "Death and life are in the power of the tongue: and they that love it shall eat the fruit thereof. "

When you speak them out loud, your spirit hears your words and believes them. That action alone grows your faith. Especially when we speak God's words from the Bible.

Our words are powerful, and everything in our environment responds to our words. If you speak positive things and believe them, then you will see good things happen in your life. If you say negative things, you will see bad things happen in your life.

Did you know that you can talk yourself to death? If you always say stuff like That just kills me, That scares me to death, I would have a heart attack, I would just die, etc., Your spirit hears those words, and your words have the power to make those things happen. It could actually kill you if you speak it long enough. If your words are always negative, your life will bear the fruit of it.

Your words are seeds into your life. If you want to live a miserable life, continue to speak negative things. If you want to live an awesome life. Be positive in your thoughts and let it reflect in your words.

When you pray, Jesus intercedes for you with God and starts the wheels turning to answer your prayer. Your angels are commanded to go and make your wishes or words happen.

God and your angels respond to your words. Be careful what you say. You get what you ask for.

CHAPTER 7

When you are saved, God's spirit comes to live inside of you. You are given God's faith right then.

Romans 12:3 (KJV) says, "For I say, through the grace given unto me, to every man that is among you, not to think himself more highly than he ought to think, but to think soberly, according as God hath dealt to every man the measure of faith."

We as Christians were all given the same measure of faith. I wasn't given more faith than anyone else, and no one was given more faith than me.

What differs from each of us is how we use our faith. You have to realize what you have to use it effectively.

Jesus said with faith the size of a mustard seed, you can move mountains. So, you don't need big faith, but you need faith without unbelief.

Matthew 17:20, KJV, says, "And Jesus said unto them, Because of your unbelief: for verily I say unto you, if ye have faith as a grain of mustard seed, ye shall say unto this mountain, remove hence to yonder place; and it shall move; and nothing shall be impossible unto you."

If your faith is weak or you feel like you don't have any faith, don't worry; there is help. You need to renew your mind with God's word.

Read the scriptures and study their meaning. Find a good commentary and grow your knowledge. Increased knowledge equals increased faith. The more Jesus that you get into your mind, the less Satan can be there.

***

Romans 12:2, KJV, says, "And be not conformed to this world: but be ye transformed by the renewing of your mind, that ye may prove what is that good and acceptable and perfect will of God.

Another thing that is important in getting faith to work for you. You must believe. We have a part in receiving our miracles from God. You have to believe that you will receive it. You have to have faith and not doubt.

God is Good
All-Ways and Always!

In Matthew 13:58 KJV, it says, "And he did not do many mighty works there because of their unbelief."

That was talking about Jesus not being able to heal and bless everyone because they didn't have faith to receive. It was his desire to heal them and bless them, but they didn't believe it, so it limited his power to do so.

You need to realize that you are the only reason that you haven't received your miracle.

God is willing. Jesus paid for it, but you have to believe it and receive it by faith. Don't doubt in your heart, and don't quit believing until you get it!

CHAPTER 8

We are living in different times, unusual times for me because I have lived through times that are better and times that have been worse. The last few years have been some of the worst times in my life.

That statement is a view of the natural, and if we were stuck living in the natural, it would be a pretty grim outlook and future for us, but praise God that's not our only choice! God gave us more.

We all have choices in life. You can choose what you wear, eat, say, think, and do. That is a God-given freedom. You can choose to do right or wrong. You have free will from God.

What is in your heart determines the choices that you make. You can choose God's way and live an awesome, blessed life. You don't have to live in this world defeated and at the mercy of the devil.

God is Good
All-Ways and Always!

You have been given grace and mercy from God so that in this fallen world you have a hope and a future! You can live in perfect peace right here on earth, just as there is peace in heaven!

Throughout this book I am going to share some personal experiences that will back up what I'm saying based on my experiences.

I have learned these principles firsthand. They are not just teachings that I have read from the Bible; they are real events in my life, and I want to share them with you so that you can relate to them and know that if God blessed me, he will certainly bless you too.

Our victories become testimonies, and that gives other people hope when they're facing similar circumstances. I am trying to give you hope because I know what Jesus did for me; he will do for you.

CHAPTER 9

I've learned that I have control that I didn't know I had and that I didn't know how to use…until I did!!

That's when everything changed for me, and I'm going to share it with you to let you know it'll work for you too. If you apply it in your life.

What am I talking about? Right now, you're thinking she's gone mad!! Should I just put the book down, or should I continue just to see how crazy she really is? Just keep reading. I promise it'll change your life if you let it; it's your choice.

What I am talking about is the law of faith. Yes, there is a law of faith. If you ask and believe that you receive, then you do.

Let me go ahead and say this: faith works if you use it. If you don't use faith, you are absolutely right—faith doesn't work! When you hear about someone being blessed or healed and you say, "That will never happen to me," you are absolutely right! It won't! Your words have power, and they come to pass.

If you are happy for others when they're blessed, it gives you hope. Then you say if it happened for them, it can happen for me too. You are absolutely right—it will!

I was always afraid of dreaming for things throughout my life because I didn't want to go through the disappointment if I didn't get them. That has hindered blessings from coming to me. I didn't have hope for my prayers to be answered. I couldn't imagine receiving what I had asked for; therefore, I didn't get it. It was a complete lack of faith on my part! It was total disbelief because I didn't believe that God would actually provide things for me. Part of it was ignorance, and part was just fear.

When you pray, believe that you receive. Imagine receiving the thing that you are hoping for. Have faith and believe without seeing what you are praying for.

If it's a new car. Imagine the make, model, and color of it. See yourself driving it; see it parked in your driveway. Put a picture in your mind of what you desire to make it real in your imagination.

Faith, belief, and hope all work together. They are all necessary to receive your blessing.

CHAPTER 10

I have learned that you can trust God every time and in every area of your life!

When you get that bad report from the doctor or any other area of your life—finances, work, family, etc.—if the prognosis is not good. You may think that you are powerless to what the devil is trying to do to you, but you're not.

Remember, everything bad comes from Satan! Everything good comes from God, right?!

Don't be afraid because I know a man, Jesus Christ. He gave his life so that you could have life more abundantly, and he gave you the power to defeat the devil no matter what he is throwing at you or on you!

The Bible says, "The thief cometh not but to steal, and kill, and destroy. I am come that they might have life and have it more abundantly." John 10:10, KJV.

God is Good
All-Ways and Always!

The thief is the devil, and he's going to start telling you now that what I am saying is a lie because that's his game.

He wants you in unbelief because then faith can't work in your life!

The I am in that verse is the great man, Jesus, who gave it all because he knew we needed a savior and he was the only way for us to survive this world and make it to the next destination, heaven.

Without Jesus we would surely be facing every curse that the enemy wants to put on us while we live on earth, and then we would still go to hell when we die!

Thank you, Jesus, for your life and your sacrifice. Because of you, we can face each day with renewed strength and assurance that we have the power to defeat Satan through our faith in you!

CHAPTER 11

The faith that I am talking about cannot be halfway; it has to be all in, or you will not get the results that you desire!

In the Bible it says, "But let him ask in faith, nothing wavering. For he that wavereth is like a wave of the sea driven with the wind and tossed. For let not that man think that he should receive anything of the Lord. A double-minded man is unstable in all his ways" (James 1:6-8, KJV).

What is that really saying? When you choose to believe God's word and stand on his promises in the Bible. You have to believe with your whole heart, have childlike faith.

You know children are so precious and innocent, and they are the closest thing to God we will see on this earth.

They are not corrupted yet, and their spirits are pure, so when you tell a child something, they have no reason not to believe you.

That is the kind of faith we have to have, and it's doable.

It does take a little more effort because, unlike children, we have been exposed to more evil, and we have been taught that God is ruthless and he's just waiting on you to mess up so that he can smack you down, right? Wrong!

I believed that for years, but I have gotten to know God, and he is absolutely good! Robin D. Bullock (an awesome prophet of God) penned that line, and it's true!

To help you start to believe that God is good, let's talk about it some more.

God is love; he sent his

Son to teach us how to live on this earth and to die for us. There had to be atonement for our sins, and Jesus shed his blood for us so that we wouldn't have to die for our sins and go to hell.

Jesus came to earth; he lived a perfect life, although he had all of the temptations that we face as humans living on this earth. He chose not to sin.

In order for him to cover our sin, he couldn't have sin in his life. He had to be perfect, and he was!

The greatest thing that he did was to accept our punishment for our sin. It's like a sibling or a friend taking a punishment that you were supposed to get. Who does that? Jesus did!

CHAPTER 12

Our world is composed of laws; God created all of them. He allowed men to discover them, but they are God's laws. There are physical laws such as the law of gravity, attraction, rhythm, relativity, and cause and effect, just to name a few.

There are natural laws, such as the law of divine oneness, that state we are all connected by our creator, God! Like it or not, believe it or not, it's the truth. The reason that people are miserable and feel disconnected in this world is because they are denying this law in their lives.

They are running from any connection with God instead of running to their creator. The one who knows how many hairs are on their head and everything else about them.

There is a law of vibration that says everything in the universe has frequency and vibration; nothing ever stands still, everything is always pushed away or pulled toward something, and you can attract things or change things by frequency. Our words have sound, and sound creates frequency, and everything in our world responds to that frequency, especially ... your words. Your words have power!

I know that you have heard about people talking to their plants, and no doubt you've read about experiments done with plants. When the person would speak kind words to their plants, the plants would just flourish and be so beautiful and healthy, but when they spoke harshly and unkindly, the plants would die. Side note: here everything responds this way too, especially people!

There have also been experiments done with water that when the water was spoken to harshly and put in the freezer, it formed disorganized asymmetrical structures, but when it was spoken to kindly, it formed the most beautiful symmetrical structures. That's proof that words matter and that things in our world respond to our spoken word.

So, I have said all of this to get to this point about another law that is most important, and when applied in your life, it will change your world!

God is Good
All-Ways and Always!

The law of faith, God created it; it's in the Bible, it's God's law, and he intended for us to use it to live here on earth.

The law of faith guarantees that when we apply it to our life, it works every time!

The law of faith says that when we pray, if we believe, we will receive what we ask for. God's answer is always yes and amen to his children.

You can trust God every time because he never changes. He is the same yesterday, today, and forever.

His words are true too! That means every promise in the Bible is for you as much as it was for people when Jesus walked the earth.

CHAPTER 13

God doesn't cause things to happen to us, although most people believe that he does because they think he controls everything in the universe and in our lives.

It's simply not true! God gave Adam authority over everything when he created him.

"And God said, Let us make man in our image, after our likeness: and let him have dominion over the fish of the sea, and over the fowl of the air, and over the cattle, and over all the earth, and over every creeping thing that creepeth upon the earth." Genesis 1:26, KJV.

Adam had authority until he sinned, and he gave his authority over to Satan when he disobeyed God's command to not eat of the fruit of the forbidden tree.

So, we're living in a fallen world, and people are looking for something, anything, to dull the pain of life!

God is Good
All-Ways and Always!

The truth is that our spirits instinctively know that we need a relationship with God, but our minds and bodies don't always cooperate.

What happens is an internal conflict that makes us miserable. We know something is missing, so we seek things to fill that void.

Remember how I said earlier that something was missing in me and that I had a void? This was it!

We look for peace, love, joy, and happiness in all of the things of this world.

We abuse food, alcohol, drugs, and sex, seeking to fill the emptiness inside of us.

Which is just our spirit longing to have a relationship with God.

We spend a lifetime trying to fix all the broken things in our life.

When all we really need to do is draw close to God through Jesus, our lives would be so amazing.

I wished that I had learned this earlier in my life. I wasted years struggling and stressing when I didn't have to.

I have tried to make it on my own, to be my own advisor and provider.

That is not the way to live. I created some big messes.

That's why I'm writing this book to teach you that there is a better way to live.

I've spent years researching faith and trusting in God.

God has all the answers, and God has given us all of the answers that we need to not just survive this world but to live abundantly!

"The thief cometh not, but to steal, and to kill, and to destroy: I am come that they might have life and that they might have it more abundantly." John 10:10, KJV.

The they in that verse is you, and the might means that it's contingent on you accepting Jesus as your savior and living under the kingdom laws.

The Bible is the living word of God, and it's as alive today as when it was first written!

The Bible was written by man, but it was inspired by the Holy Spirit from God, and every word is true; you can count on it. In fact, I advise it.

Don't keep struggling in this life when you don't have to.

"Jesus cried and said, 'He that believeth on me, believeth not on me, but on him that sent me. And he that seeth me seeth him that sent me. I am come a light into the world, that whosoever believeth on me should not abide in darkness." John 12:44-46; KJV.

That's a promise right there. Trust God and believe in Jesus; he's the son of the living God, and you will not abide in darkness in this world!

Take it from someone who has had many failures along the way because I was trying to do everything on my own.

What a mess I made at times!

That's the way most people live. I did until God revealed to me that there is a better way, and it's easy and free to us.

We just have to believe. If God had wanted you to wing it on your own, he wouldn't have written a guidebook, the Bible.

CHAPTER 14

The dictionary defines faith" as complete trust in someone or something.

The Bible says faith is the substance of things hoped for, the evidence of things not seen. (Hebrews 11:1, KJV)

So, faith is complete trust in God for everything, even when you cannot see the thing you're trusting for.

The Bible says, "And Jesus answering saith unto them, Have faith in God. For verily I say unto you, that whosoever shall say unto this mountain, Be thou removed and be thou cast into the sea," and shall not doubt in his heart, but shall believe that those things which he saith shall come to pass, he shall have whatsoever he saith. Therefore I say unto you, What things soever ye desire, when ye pray, believe that ye receive them, and ye shall have them." Mark 11:22-24; KJV.

That verse is stating how faith works. If you believe you receive, and if you don't, you won't, plain and simple!

"And all things, whatsoever ye shall ask in prayer, believing, ye shall receive." Matthew 21:22; KJV.

All things that you ask in prayer, believing, you receive. It didn't say maybe or sometimes either. It just said, Ask in prayer, believe, and receive!

Those are Jesus' words, not mine! Faith is a law that God created!

CHAPTER 15

Before I get into how faith works, let's start from the beginning so that you can really understand why it will work! Why do we have spiritual authority in our lives?

The first story in the Bible is the story of God creating everything. I will add here that God created everything by speaking it into existence. He released His words in faith; he spoke them out loud. He created the world, the universe, the animals, the plants, people, and everything.

So, In the beginning there was just God, but he wanted a family, so he decided to create us. In order for us to live, we had to have a place to live and things to keep us alive, so he created light, dark, earth, water, animals, and plants necessary to sustain our lives.

God is Good
All-Ways and Always!

God's idea was that we would live in a paradise on earth, so he created a beautiful garden called Eden. God fully intended that we would live in that garden forever and just be his family. He loves us and wants to spend time with us as families do. He visited Adam and Eve in the garden every day.

The first two humans he created were Adam, a man, and his wife, Eve, a woman. God gave Adam the job of taking care of the garden; he had to maintain what God had created. God gave Adam dominion over all of his creation—angels, plants, animals, everything.

The garden was also a place of protection; therefore, Adam and Eve didn't wear clothes, but because their world was sinless, they didn't know they were naked. They were allowed to eat the fruit from the tree of life, and that fruit would ensure that they would live forever.

They had it made in that garden; it was paradise. Everything was provided for them, and the only thing they had to do was love God, spend time with him, and obey his law.

You know most people don't like to obey authority; we're born with a sin nature. It is a sin to disobey God. You would've thought that it would have been easy to obey the one who gave you life and everything to sustain that life, but that's not how it worked out.

Everything was going well. Adam and Eve were living like a king and a queen. They lived in peace, they were never sick, they didn't have pain, and everything they needed was provided for them. They would've been able to live like that forever. They could've had children, raised their family, and continued to live in the garden and have it all.

Adam and Eve had freedom to roam about freely in the garden. God also gave them free choice in deciding what they would do in their lives.

God visited them often, but he didn't rule over them because he loved them too much to do that, so he allowed them to make their own choices in life, just like us. We have freedom to choose everything in our life.

The trees in the Garden of Eden were beautiful and provided plenty of food for them. God told them that they could eat as much as they wanted from every tree except the tree of knowledge of good and of evil.

He told them not to eat from this tree, or they would die. That sounds easy enough, right?

God is Good
All-Ways and Always!

Now let me tell you about another spirit that walked in the garden. We call him Satan. He was once a beautiful angel, in fact the most beautiful angel God ever created; his name was Lucifer. Lucifer wasn't happy just being one of God's angels; he wanted to be greater than God, and he wanted everyone to worship him instead of God.

Satan tried to convince other angels to follow him and worship him, and some did. God cast Satan and all of his evil followers out of heaven, so Satan set out to destroy God's creation on this earth.

He decided if he could get man to worship him, he would be greater than God. Satan went into the garden where Adam and Eve lived, and he started trying to convince Eve that God had lied to them. He eventually convinced Adam and Eve to eat the fruit of the tree of knowledge, good and evil, because he knew that God would be upset with them and that a curse would come on them and everyone after them! Remember that Satan wanted them to worship him, so he was very convincing and conniving, just the way he is today in our lives.

He tries to make you believe that God doesn't care about you, that he really doesn't mean what he said in the Bible. That faith doesn't work. That none of this applies to you. That it's not real.

Remember that I told you that he is seeking to steal, kill, and destroy, always! He is the author of lies and confusion; if he can get you to doubt, then your faith can't work, and he knows that.

He paints sin as pretty and fun; he tells you that it's just a little sin. Well, the truth is that sin is sin. No matter which sins you commit, they're all wrong.

What he doesn't tell you is that our sins rob us of blessings that God wants us to have. There are degrees of sin; all sin is wrong, but there are sins worse than others, but no sin goes unpunished!

Every sin is punishable by death, but remember who paid that price: Jesus! You have a hope and a future because of him.

The only unforgivable sin is not accepting Jesus Christ as your savior and believing that he died for our sin. He rose again the third day, after he defeated Satan, death, hell, and the grave.

The sin that Adam and Eve committed was that they trusted Satan over God.

God removed his protection and blessings from Adam, Eve, and all of us after them. This is when the curse came on the earth. Adam's authority over everything that God created was handed over to Satan, so therefore he became ruler of this world.

They were forced out of the garden, and from that point on they felt the consequences of sin. They had to work for food and shelter; they became sick and felt pain, and for the first time they knew they would die. They no longer had the promise to live forever in the garden, but most importantly, they lost fellowship with God!

Life wasn't easy anymore. Let me say, before you go hating on them, we have to ask ourselves, what would we have done? In our lives we are faced with choices to sin or not sin. How often do you choose to sin when you know it's wrong? I know I have chosen to sin even when I knew I shouldn't. So, I am saying that although this story is disappointing, I can't cast any stones!

I have some good news for you, though. God had a plan in which we could be redeemed from the curse.

Before I get into that, let me go back and say that in the Old Testament of the Bible, after Adam and Eve sinned against God, No one could talk directly to God.

God no longer visited with Adam and Eve. You had to be a high priest, and they had to follow a lot of rules and rituals and provide pure sacrifices to God to atone for their sin and the sin of the people. Only then could the priest talk to God on behalf of the people.

There was not a communication directly from people to God until Jesus.

God requires an atonement for sin, and that was death. That's why the animals had to be pure and blemish-free; they couldn't be sick or injured. They had to be as perfect a specimen as possible, but they were never good enough to truly atone for our sins and make things right between man and God.

God loved us, and he didn't want to have the separation between us and

him. He missed the closeness that he had with Adam and Eve, and he wanted his family back. He wanted us to be able to talk with him directly, so he had a plan to save us.

God's plan to redeem us from the curse was for his son Jesus to come to earth in the form of a human (man) and to live on earth. To teach us God's ways. To teach us about faith, healing, blessing, and cursing. Jesus was God in the flesh who came to earth by divine conception; his mother was a young Jewish woman named Mary, but his father was God through the Holy Spirit.

You may have trouble believing that, but just remember we're talking about God. The divine creator of the universe and everything in it, including you!

You see, God loves us despite our sins and failures. He hates our sin, but he loves us. So, he gave his son for us. Jesus came to bring that message to us, but his ultimate purpose was to die for us.

You remember that I said that pure animals had to be sacrificed to atone for our sin? Jesus was that pure sacrifice. He lived in a fallen world and was tempted by the devil just like we are, but he never sinned ... never!!!

CHAPTER 16

Now that we've established how God set things up and how and why it works, We have also revealed the mystery of living a blessed, abundant life here on earth.

I will share some of my personal experiences and testimonies with you.

I have many things to share because I have been through some stuff! I will not be able to share everything in this book, but maybe in the next one.

I have almost died at least 3-4 times in my life. I will share just a few.

No doubt there are more that will be revealed to me in heaven. Times when my angels intervened in life-threatening situations that I wasn't even aware of. All of us have those close calls that we don't even know about until God tells us in heaven one day.

God is Good
All-Ways and Always!

When your plans get changed or you get delayed. Remember to thank God for it because it could be our angels protecting us from God only knows what. It might be frustrating, but there was a reason for it. There aren't any coincidences; those are divine interventions.

The first time that I nearly died, I was around 7-8 years old. My cousins and I were going to the local movie theater. We had to cross a busy 4-lane highway in order to get there. My mom and my aunt were standing with us to tell us when it was safe to cross. I was so excited to get to the theater that I just bolted. I didn't look for cars; I just wanted to get to the other side of that highway so that we could get to the theater sooner.

Suddenly I just stopped in my tracks. In the middle of the road. I had run out in front of a car going at a high rate of speed. I turned and stared at the car as it was approaching. It was all in slow motion right then. Brakes were squealing, tires were smoking, and my mom was screaming.

The car suddenly came to a stop, and my face was inches away from the front grill. I literally thought my life was over. There was only one reason that that car was able to stop; it had to be supernatural. It was too close and going too fast to stop on its own.

It defied Newton's second law of physics. A car going 55 mph would require 250-300 feet to stop. That car stopped in a distance of about 20 feet. That's impossible with the law of physics, but with God all things are possible.

My legs were like rubber right then. I couldn't move. My mom came out to get me, and the man got out of his car cursing and screaming. His legs were like rubber also, I'm sure. It was such a close call!

I didn't realize that God had saved me that day, but looking back, I know he did. I am grateful for that, although my life has not always been easy at times. I am glad that God spared me so that I could live it. I have lived long enough to learn how awesome God is and that God is good all ways and always!

CHAPTER 17

My next close call was during childbirth. My oldest son came into this world half-grown. He was a whopping 10 lbs.!

Throughout the labor and delivery, I was hemorrhaging slightly. When it came time to deliver, I hemorrhaged a lot! In the delivery room, which back then was set up like an operating room. It had big, huge lights that allowed the doctors and nurses to see everything clearly.

As the baby was born, I lost my sight; I was blind. The blood loss was so great that I couldn't see anything. It was dark to me. I couldn't even make out silhouettes. When he was born, they laid him up on my stomach, and they said, Look, he's so big. I tried but couldn't see.

I didn't know his sex for sure, so I asked, "What is it, a boy or a girl?" " I can't see."

They realized the gravity of the situation, and they literally pushed my mom out of the room. She told me that when she looked back, I was gushing blood.

They kept slapping me in the face and telling me to stay awake. I didn't know what was going on, but I felt horrible. I was so weak.

Over the next couple of days, I learned that I had hemorrhaged so much that they had to give me 3 units of blood.

I spent a longer time in the hospital than normal, but the baby and I came out healthy. That was God being good as always!

CHAPTER 18

The next incident was the most traumatic! I was in my early 30s. I was a wife, a mom, and a nurse. My schedule was busy, and I was very tired. I had gone to my doctor just to get a checkup.

They discovered that I had enlarged lymph nodes in my chest through a chest X-ray. I was driving home from that appointment when my doctor called and said, Come back. We needed to do a CT scan to confirm their findings, and they scheduled a biopsy right away.

The surgeon decided to go in with a scope and obtain tissue for biopsy. I'm not exactly sure what transpired, but somehow, he didn't biopsy a lymph node, but he took a bite out of an artery in my chest cavity.

He came out to my husband and told him that he needed to open my chest up to go in and take care of some "cloudiness in there ". He meant bleeding, but those weren't his words.

Of course, my husband agreed. He told him to "do what you need to do ".

So, the surgery became a thoracotomy. It's a big surgery. They enter your chest wall through your ribs and collapse your lung in order to access the area that they need to operate on.

Later the doctor came out and told my husband that he got the biopsy and I was doing good. He said that I would be brought out to the recovery room eventually and that he could come in and see me. My husband said it was taking too long, and he knew something wasn't right.

I also knew something wasn't right as I laid in the recovery room. I was half awake. My body didn't feel right! It wasn't just post-op pain and discomfort either. There was something wrong!

I listened to everything going on around me, and as a nurse, I was trying to determine what was wrong. My body was so weak, breathing was difficult. I couldn't say anything or ask for help. I didn't have the strength to get the words out of my mouth.

One of the nurses checked my blood pressure, and it was dropping rapidly. She alerted the team. They determined that I was going back into surgery to find and repair internal bleeding. My blood pressure was dropping and eventually dropped to 50/20 before they got me back in. That's not enough pressure to sustain life. I was about to crash, and they knew it.

Before rushing me back in, they let my husband, brother, and sister-in-law in to see me.

They described me as grotesque. My body was so swollen from fluids that they were pushing to keep my blood pressure up that I had 50 lbs of extra weight on me.

The only thing that I managed to speak to my husband when they came in was, "Don't tell the kids how bad."

I could only think about how devastated my little boys would be if I didn't come home. I didn't want them to worry and me not to be there to comfort them. I was determined to survive! I would not leave them to face this world without me.

While my family was standing there. A doctor came in and started grabbing IV bags that had pressure cuffs on them that were forcing fluids into me. He threw them on the bed, unlocked the wheels, and started to run with me to the OR.

When they wheeled me back into the operating room. I was aware of my surroundings. I thought it was strange because most of the time when you go into surgery, you are at least slightly sedated to the point where you don't really see the operating room.

I thought this was odd, but I expected to be sedated any second. That didn't happen.

My blood pressure was so low that the anesthesiologist could not sedate me. Anesthesia lowers your blood pressure, and I was on the bottom already.

Anesthesia would have killed me. So, he had to make the decision to let me live but go through the most torturous thing anyone could go through. Surgery without anesthesia!!

He could only paralyze me so that I would not move, but I couldn't have anything to sedate me or for pain.

As the surgery began, I was screaming to them that I was awake. You didn't put me to sleep! I was screaming at the top of my lungs to Stop!!!!!

Please stop, but no sound was coming out!!!

I was fully aware of the cutting, burning, and sounds. I didn't understand why they weren't stopping. I tried to move my body. I wanted to jump up, but I couldn't move.

The pain was unbearable! The incision on my back is approximately 8 inches long. It curves and goes under my left arm. My ribs were separated, and my lung collapsed. All of this was done while I was awake.

My mind was reeling! Why didn't they put me to sleep?

As a nurse, I knew there was a phenomenon called awareness during surgery. It's where they gave you anesthesia to put you to sleep, and to the anesthesiologist, it appears that you are asleep, but you're not! You are aware of everything, and you feel everything!

That was the only thing that I could come up with at that time. I must have awareness!

I believe the records show it was over an hour into the procedure before the doctor could actually sedate me.

When I woke up in the intensive care unit. I was in incredible pain. This pain was not just from the surgical incision or chest tubes.

My whole body was hurting from experiencing so much blood loss because when you have significant blood loss, your tissues are starved of oxygen, and it's extremely painful.

The worst pain that I felt was in my left arm. I couldn't understand why it hurt so bad! I'm not a wimp when it comes to pain either. I have a high pain threshold, and I can tolerate a lot, but this pain was over the top. There are no words to describe it!

It was the main thing that I asked the nurses to help me with. I was trying to figure out why it hurt so bad. I was thinking the chest tubes must be pushing on a nerve or something, but I didn't know how.

When I was able to speak, I told my family about the awareness that I had in surgery. They listened but thought I had hallucinated, that there is no way that happened.

It wasn't until the anesthesiologist asked me if I recalled anything from the surgery that they believed me.

I said yes that I had awareness! He said, "No, you didn't."

He proceeded to tell me that my blood pressure had dropped so low (50/20) that he was unable to put me to sleep because it would have killed me. He had tears in his eyes as he spoke. He said it was the hardest thing that he had to do in 31 years of his career, but it was absolutely necessary.

I thanked him for making that decision that day. I thanked him that I was still here to be with my family and raise my boys. I thank God for leading him to make that decision! My angels were on the job telling him to save her life!

It was a horrific experience, and there are no words to describe it. I can remember all of it to this day, but if I had been given the choice, I would've chosen to live also, no matter what I had to go through for it.

As my recovery progressed, my left arm pain didn't improve. I was almost out of my mind with the intense burning. stabbing and shooting pain! It hurt so bad that you couldn't touch it. Air passing over it even hurt it!

I was asking every doctor that came in about it, but I wasn't getting answers. Eventually a neurologist came in to see me and explained that this sometimes happens with the particular procedure that I had, a thoracotomy. She went on to say that all should be resolved in 6 months.

I thought, are you kidding me?! 6 months of this? Ok, I will make it 6 months, and I will be back to normal, and the pain will be gone. I can do that!

Little did I know, but it was going to be 13 years of this. It changed my life and my family's life. It was so debilitating at times that I could hardly function.

I went to every doctor imaginable looking for help, but they all had the same message: there isn't a cure for this. I didn't know about Jesus Cure at the time; I didn't know I had faith or how to use it yet.

The good news was that I didn't have lymphoma, but the bad news was that I had a brachial plexus injury that resulted in reflex sympathetic dystrophy.

To put it plainly, I hurt like heck!! My arm felt like it was in an oven baking while someone was beating it with a hammer and trying to pull it off at the same time! It felt like the skin was pulled off and you were pouring alcohol over it! It felt like you were driving nails in it! It felt like a toothache throbbing and shooting nerve pain up and down my arm with spasms. Every pain sensation that we had was in my arm all the time.

I had to immobilize it to help with the pain. Movement made all of the symptoms worse. So, I wore a sling to protect it because touching it was unbearable.

After years of pain medication around the clock. Only being able to sleep 2-3 hours at a time before being woken up in pain. I continued to seek help.

I wasn't close to God at this time, and I had no idea that he would heal me. I didn't know that Jesus paid for my healing, so I didn't know to ask for it or claim it. I suffered for a long time that I didn't have to.

I met a man one day who asked me about my arm. I told him that I had RSD (reflex sympathetic dystrophy); he quickly told me that he did too once.

My ears perked up, and I asked, What do you mean you had it? He shared that he had gone to acupuncture and that his pain was gone; he no longer suffered with it.

I started acupuncture the next day! To make a very long story short, I went for about 4 years weekly. I could tell a difference almost immediately, but after so many years of nerve damage, there was a lot to overcome through the treatment.

I received my healing at that time, like I said earlier. I didn't know that God was the healer, but I know very well now, and no matter where the healing comes from. Whether it's a doctor or medicine, it ultimately comes from God through Jesus! I was told that there was no cure, but doctors don't know everything if they don't know about our God and our Jesus!

God gave doctors and surgeons the knowledge to understand the body and develop procedures and medicine to heal us, but without him we would not be healed.

Jesus paid for our healing, but we have to believe it and accept it by faith to receive it.

1 Peter 2:24, KJV, says, "Who his own self bare our sins in his own body on the tree, that we, being dead to sins, should live unto righteousness: by whose stripes we were healed."

That verse says we were healed; we are not waiting to be healed. We are already healed, but you have to cooperate to receive it.

How do you do that? Just believe it! Have faith even if nothing changes in the natural. If the symptoms are still there or are getting worse, keep believing! Faith works every time!

Everything that happened to me medically was an attack from Satan. I didn't know that for many years.

In fact, I thought all of that pain and suffering came from God. I thought it was happening to make me stronger or be a better Christian.

Looking back, that is some warped thinking! How do sickness and suffering glorify God?

If a parent hurts their child intentionally, do you think more of them? Do you tell people what a great person that they are? Do you want to be closer to them? Do you sing their praises? No, of course not!

Then why would you think that God intentionally hurts you or makes you sick? God is our father.

I'm sure that God wishes that everyone would stop accusing him of doing such things.

All good things come from God. If it's good, it's God, and if it's bad, it's the devil.

Embed this into your mind; renew your mind to accept it. It will help you to believe it, and then you can start receiving all of the blessings that God wants you to have.

CHAPTER 19

As I stated earlier, I really began to study God's word. I wanted to understand it. I wanted to know why some people received healing and others did not. Although I would hear them say with all conviction that their faith was in God for their healing.

I have heard people say that God is in control. Whatever God's will is for them, that's what they wanted. If I am supposed to be sick or die, to God be the glory.

Ok, hold up! Let's stop right here. I don't even want you thinking those thoughts. Those are words of unbelief.

It's not God's will for you to be sick or die until your numbered days are up! God wants you well!

You cannot fully serve him if you are sick. You can't serve anyone, yourself or your family either. We are

God's workers here on earth. We are his vessels that he performs miracles through.

Do not accept sickness as being a badge of honor to wear because you think it's from God. It's from the devil! If you accept it, you're honoring him, not God!

I'm very passionate about healing because I got a revelation from God's word, and I am not letting go.

God told me to tell you about it and how I was healed more than once. I still get healed as quickly as something tries to come on me. I start speaking to it and my body.

I claim my healing in Jesus' name because I can. Jesus paid for it, and by his stripes we were healed. 1 Peter 2:24; KJV.

If we were healed, then we are healed every time. We don't have to beg God to heal us. He's already given us everything that we need to be healed.

It's up to us to receive it through faith. You are not waiting on God; he's waiting on you!

Jesus took on every sickness known to man. He took all of it into his body and into the grave. He defeated all of it by this act. He arose healthy and whole.

So, we as Christians can claim our healing now and use his healing power to make us whole.

Jesus is the name above every name, so you have to speak out of your mouth, out loud. Tell whatever sickness you have to leave in Jesus' name.

Use your words; you can't read it or think it has to be spoken. Speak to the mountain (problem) in your life. Whether it's your health, finances, family issues, marital problems, etc.

You have to speak words out in faith, believing that you receive when you speak them. Believe what you say and say what you believe.

Our words have power, whether they are positive or negative. Choose your words wisely.

Faith works for all healing in every area of your life. It's a law that God made, and it will not fail if used properly. When you understand this, you don't doubt it.

When you use your words and take authority over any situation/problem (mountain) in your life. When you truly believe that Jesus paid for this and don't doubt, then you receive it. You get what you say.

Don't speak to God about your problem. Speak to your problem about your God.

God is Good
All-Ways and Always!

Jesus is the name above every name. So in the name of Jesus, cancer be gone, body be healed, mind be healed, bank account be healed, and marriage be restored. Satan, take your hands off of me and my family. You have no authority in my life.

You have authority because Jesus paid for you to have it. That's why he suffered and died for us. He took every attack that we will have spiritually, physically, mentally, emotionally, and financially to the grave, and when he rose again, he defeated all of it.

There isn't a problem that he didn't overcome. The only problem that we have is believing it and having faith to receive it.

CHAPTER 20

The biggest near-death experience came subtly. I was not expecting it. It was growing inside of me, and I had no clue until it reared its ugly head. I mean literally too.

I had felt a thickening under my left breast, but I didn't think much of it. I have had breast reduction surgery, and I thought it was scar tissue.

In a few months it began to grow and change. I realized that it was getting bigger, but I had the revelation from God's word, and I claimed my healing.

I spoke to my mountain and commanded it to die in Jesus' name! I said, Whatever you are, you cannot stay in my body. I didn't have a diagnosis yet, but I knew it was cancer, and I called it that.

You can't deny what your problem or diagnosis is. Don't pretend it's not there; that will get you dead!

You actually have to speak to it and call it by name.

I said, Cancer, get out of my body in Jesus's name! Every bad cell be destroyed in Jesus' name! I will not accept less than complete healing in Jesus' name! I did this for months.

I will say it was not always easy to stay in faith and not get into fear. It was the first time I had actually stood on God's word like this.

I believed it would work, but I had never had a personal experience with boldly speaking about my sickness. I put my faith out for it.

The devil tried to rob me of my healing by continuing to tell me, You know you're going to die. You know that God is not going to heal you. You deserve everything that you are getting, etc.

It was a battle in my mind, and this was relatively new to me, but because it was God's words, I wasn't letting go.

You've seen pictures with the devil on one shoulder and an angel on the other one, whispering in your ear. That's exactly what it was like. Because the devil is a liar and the author of everything bad.

I chose to trust God's word and stand on his promises that if I just had faith, I would be healed.

I keep renewing my mind with the word of God. I kept believing that it was true, no matter how bad things looked.

It looked very bad. My body was showing signs that I couldn't deny. There was a growth coming out of the left side of my breast. It was the size of a lemon. It was a hideous sight, purple, red, and angry-looking.

It began to open up and drain down my left side. I had to wear a big dressing under my arm, and the drainage was so bad that I had to change it a couple of times a day.

No matter what it looked like in the natural to my eyes. I wouldn't give up my faith. I kept speaking to it to die and leave in Jesus' name. I imagined it drying up and going away.

This went on for a few months. I still hadn't gotten into a doctor because of some insurance issues, and we were in the Covid pandemic era. Everything changed during that time, but I won't elaborate here.

Anyway, my faith was strong. I understood what Jesus had done, and I was not backing down.

One morning I woke up, and when I was getting dressed, I noticed that a cross had developed on top of my left breast. It looked like it was a flesh-colored scar or tattoo. It was a perfect little cross.

I had not asked for a sign of my healing because faith requires that we believe without seeing. It doesn't take faith if you already see the end of the story. Faith pleases God, so don't be afraid to trust him; it works every time.

Although I had not asked for a sign, I believed that God gave that to me. My body did not appear healed at that point, but I knew it was, and God just confirmed my belief.

I had told my family about the cancer, and I had received the official diagnosis. Stage 4 ductal carcinoma blah, blah, blah. It was just a name because I didn't have any fear of it.

Jesus is the name above all names, and my faith was in him for my complete healing, and I would not take anything less!

So, stage 4 ductal carcinoma, you are dead, and you have to leave my body in the name of Jesus, hallelujah!!!! Amen!

I am blessed with an awesome, amazing family. My husband, two sons, two daughters-in-law, and eight grandchildren. I am blessed!!!

I knew my faith was up for my healing. I wasn't sure if their faith would be.

The whole faith thing was fairly new to me too. I mean, putting my whole trust in someone that I couldn't see or audibly hear took a lot of courage.

I had been studying God's word for a few years and specifically healing for over a year. So, I didn't know where my family was in their beliefs, but I didn't want them to get into unbelief.

When the doctor gave the diagnosis. I immediately told my family not to go looking on the internet because it would put them in fear. The internet was going to tell them that with this diagnosis. I couldn't be healed.

Fear is the exact opposite of faith. I would have been in fear myself if I had not been renewing my mind with God's word and seeking God's promises on faith and healing.

I was prepared for whatever the doctor said. I knew that no matter what he said or what my body felt like or looked like, I was healed! I would not let go of that because God promised it and Jesus paid for it. All I had to do was believe it to receive it.

This all began during the COVID era, like I mentioned earlier. You all remember this time well. Everyone's world changed. People were not going to work and were psychological prisoners in their homes.

The government incited fear in the people because they made you believe that you would die if you left your home.

If you stood within 6 feet of a person, you could catch a deadly disease, but if you walked into a restaurant and sat down, you could unmask.

Somehow, just sitting down, you were in an invisible barrier so you were safe from this "deadly" virus that knew not to cross the 6-foot barrier or affect you at the restaurant table.

Sounds ridiculous now, doesn't it? It was ridiculous then too!

They just scared people in order to control them.

I know that people died, but if you haven't realized that they didn't have to, you haven't seen the truth.

There was a treatment available that they blocked people from receiving. I personally know of lives saved by people who received the proper treatment.

I have a whole soapbox on this subject, but I will save this for another time.

Because this all happened during the COVID era, no one could go in with me for doctor appointments, chemo treatments, radiation treatments, or surgeries.

My heart hurt because my family couldn't be by my side, but I knew they were with me in their prayers, hearts, and minds. They were as physically close as they were allowed to be. Whether that was in a lobby, in the car in the parking lot, or at their work.

It was hard on them and me, but I took their love and support through those sliding doors and faced the dragon (Satan), and I had Jesus with me always.

Family, love, and support are so important for healing, and I was blessed to have so much of it!!

I love my family with all my heart, and I thank them for always being there for me!

God had prepared me for this battle because I renewed my mind with his word.

I would not let Satan kill me with this disease. I had Jesus' power in me, and his name is above all names!!

I had experienced a friend's battle with cancer just a year prior. She was a strong Christian; she believed in God for her healing, but she would state that God gave her cancer, and if it was his will for her, then she was happy with it.

You know by now that was a wrong belief. She didn't understand what she was saying, and she didn't have a revelation from God's word about healing.

The last time that I saw her, we all laid hands on her and prayed, but I knew she wasn't going to live because the light was gone out of her eyes.

By the time that I fully understood the healing revelation, she died that week.

CHAPTER 21

At the first appointment with the oncologist, he called in several doctors to look at me.

The growth was very big, and it looked pretty hideous.

Although it looked bad, they were not seeing it when it was at its worst! By this time, it was shrinking, probably the size of a walnut, and it was black like a prune and shriveled up. lol! I knew it was dead!

I could tell by the look on their faces that in their eyes this was really bad.

They began to say that we can't promise you anything, but we will do the best that we can to save you.

I said, Don't worry. I know I am healed. Jesus has healed me!!

They looked at me like I had three heads. lol!

God is Good
All-Ways and Always!

I would not back down from my faith. I would not let myself get in fear. I would not allow unbelief in my mind because if it settled there, Satan would take advantage of it and kill me!! Every time they told me that I would get worse, I would say, No, I won't in Jesus's name; I will get better!

I knew that Jesus paid for my healing by his stripes, and I wasn't going to not believe it.

It's not that I'm a better Christian or that I have more faith than any other Christian. No, not at all!

We have all been given the same measure of faith. When you accept Jesus as your savior, his faith actually comes to live on the inside of you.

The only difference between you and me is that I learned through God's word and the Holy Spirit that I had to use my faith, or it doesn't work. So I did use it, and I got healed!

I still use my faith all the time in every situation that I need to.

If you are sitting there saying that it won't work for you. Then sadly you are absolutely right!

Faith only works when you use it. You have to believe before you see a change. You can't trust your five senses to believe because sometimes things don't change for a long time. You have to keep believing no matter what you feel, see, or hear.

When the growth was coming out of my body and draining. I didn't deny it was there. I didn't deny what it was, but I did imagine it healed. I imagined it drying up and falling off of my body, and I spoke to it that way.

I said, Cancer/growth, in the name of Jesus, you are dead and will leave my body. There will not be a sign of you left.

Jesus paid for my healing, and I received it.

CHAPTER 22

You have to use the name of Jesus when you speak to any problem in your life.

Jesus' name is the name above every name.

It's above cancer, diabetes, heart disease, lung disease, skin disease, and all diseases.

It's above poverty, scarcity, financial ruin, starvation, self-destruction, and failure.

It's above depression, mental illness, emotional distress, unhappiness, anger, bitterness, marital problems, and abuse.

Jesus' name will give you victory over any problem (mountain) in your life.

You have to put your faith out for it.

You have to speak it out of your mouth, speak directly to the problem, call it by name, and tell it to leave in Jesus' name.

Believe it in your heart to receive it.

If you don't see results right away, don't give up! When you spoke in Jesus' name, God said yes. Your problem was eradicated right then, but sometimes it takes a little time to see it in our natural realm or world.

Everything that Jesus paid for you to have is in the spiritual realm, so we have to move it into the physical realm by faith.

That's all it takes—just believe it.

If you have prayed and declared your faith and spoken to your mountain to be moved and you are not seeing results, It is not God withholding your blessing. God said yes as soon as you asked. Satan is the reason for the delay!

He is either hindering the answer to your prayer, or your faith is wavering.

You have to be convinced and don't waver in your faith.

Don't be afraid to trust God!

Because God has promised all good things for us. We have to cooperate to receive it.

If your faith is strong and you know it, then Satan is the reason for the delay.

In this case you have to deal with this through praying in tongues and fasting.

CHAPTER 23

The first chemo that I received was called "red devil." They call it that because it's blood red going in, and its blood red coming out when you urinate.

Chemo can be designed to target certain cells if they have a specific marker on them. Some cancer cells have markers, but my particular cancer was what they call triple negative. It didn't have any markers for the chemo to target.

In that case they give you chemo that kills every rapidly dividing cell, which is called "red devil" chemo.

I refused to call it "red devil," so I called it Jesus Juice!

It was red like blood, and to me it was symbolic of Jesus' blood flowing into my body and killing every bad cell but salvaging every good cell.

I thanked Jesus every time I received it, and I just thought about the healing that was coming from him.

The doctors had prepared me that as the treatments progressed, I would get sicker and sicker.

I just sat there and listened, but I was pleading the blood of Jesus on me to protect me from every symptom, discomfort, and pain.

I didn't get as sick as they said that I would. When they said you would get worse, I got better.

When they told me a procedure was going to hurt really bad, it didn't!

In fact, some procedures, if I described them to you. You would be able to feel the pain just because of the way it was done, but I didn't even feel the needles go in or anything else.

The whole process of my healing took over a year. In the beginning my faith would go up and down.

That's a normal response for trying to believe something that you cannot see and you aren't 100 percent sure is going to happen.

I told you that I had studied faith, but this was the first time that I had to use it to save my life.

God is Good
All-Ways and Always!

You cannot stay on this roller coaster with your faith and get the results that you want, though.

You have to decide to believe and not waver.

Doubt, fear, and worry are unbelief. Unbelief will not move your mountains.

Take it from me, I've lived through this. It's ok to trust God because he will not let you down.

Don't think that God's not going to do it this time or that he won't do it for you.

God loves you no matter what you've done.

Jesus paid for you to have authority to speak to your problems (mountains).

It's up to you to believe it; that's the only part that God can't do for you.

Faith is a law that God created, and it works every time!

The biggest thing that I struggled with was whether to believe in God for supernatural healing or to go to the doctor and receive medicine for my healing.

I knew I was healed regardless of the way that I would receive it.

I decided that God created doctors, procedures, and medicine. He gave them knowledge to understand the human body and to treat diseases.

All healing is supernatural from God, regardless of how you get it.

My diagnosis was stage 4 breast cancer. That means the cancer had spread into lymph nodes and other organs. In my case it was my lungs. The doctors were not giving me any hope for healing.

I was not backing down from what God's word promised me. His words said that by Jesus' stripes I was healed.

If I believed that in my heart and spoke it out of my mouth. I could have what I say!

After months of chemotherapy. I had a double mastectomy followed by 33 radiation treatments.

Following the mastectomy, all of the tissue that was removed was sent for biopsies.

When I went in for my post-op appointment. The doctor gave me the results from the biopsy reports.

He told me that there were NO cancer cells present in any tissue.

He also said, "Our medicine didn't do this! It doesn't do this!"

I said, "I know that, and I wasn't relying on your medicine. I knew before the first day that I came in here that I was healed. It was Jesus!"

The next PET scan that I had was excellent too; no sign of cancer, tumors, growths, or enlarged lymph nodes anywhere in my body.

You may not understand this, but that doesn't happen with chemotherapy. It doesn't kill every cancer cell, only the rapidly dividing ones, but the ones at rest survive.

All of the cancer cells in my body were dead!!!

All because of Jesus!!

Chapter

Since then, I have been healed supernaturally many times. I will feel a pain or symptom coming on me, and I will speak to it in the name of Jesus and believe that I'm healed, and I am every time.

I get mad if Satan tries to make me sick. If I start feeling any symptoms, I immediately start telling them to go away. I tell my body to be healed.

I speak Psalm 91 over my life.

It's a psalm of supernatural protection if you put your faith and trust in God. If you believe you receive it and you don't, you won't.

I use faith for everything in my life. It's not just for healing.

It's for family, marriage, friendship, homes, cars, and prosperity. I could go on and on.

I know I keep repeating myself, but I want you to get the revelation that I got, and if I need to say it 1000 times, I will.

Faith works if you use it; it has to work; it's God's law.

It requires that you put your trust in him for everything.

It works in every area of your life because God cares about the slightest details of your life.

He's not oblivious to your needs. He knows what you need and wants to provide everything for you, but you have a part in receiving from him.

As a Christian, you have been given all of the faith/power that you need to overcome the devil.

If you don't use the power inside of you through Jesus, then nothing changes.

God is Good
All-Ways and Always!

Bro. Andrew Wommack uses this example to make this point.

The power company runs all of the power lines to your house. Flowing through those lines is all the electricity that you need to run every electrical item in your house, including your lights.

When nighttime comes, if you do not go over and flip the switch, you will sit in the dark.

The power company is not going to come out and do that part for you.

If you call them and say, I'm in the dark, can you help me? They're going to tell you that they have given you all of the power that you need.

You already have it. It's up to you to use it; flip the switch.

You have to use the faith that you were given when you accepted Jesus as your savior.

We were all given the same amount of faith.

You have to believe it and put your trust in God to receive it. Don't be afraid because it's a law that God created, and it works every time!

If you still don't believe this, get into the word of God. Renew your mind to these truths because the devil doesn't want you to know the power that you have been given.

I'm sure he's making you doubt right now. Start speaking to him and tell him to leave you alone in the name of Jesus, and he has to go!

He has no power in your life unless you give it to him. You can use the name of Jesus on him, and he's defeated.

I hope that you understand about faith now. I am testifying to you that it works.

I trusted God's word and put my faith in Jesus.

It didn't fail me, and it won't fail you.

No matter what the devil throws at you or on you. You do not have to just take it. You have authority.

God will not force you to use your faith. He gave you free will to choose how you live your life. You can choose to believe in him and have victory in everything in your life, or you can doubt and not use your faith, and Satan will destroy you every chance that he gets.

God established this law because he knew what the devil was going to do to you. So, he gave you a way to overcome every attack.

God is Good
All-Ways and Always!

Because we are living in a fallen world, Satan is going to continue to attack us, but God gave us a way to have a blessed, victorious life.

Have faith in God and use his words. Speak to your problem in Jesus' name with the authority that you have been given. Believe that you receive it, and you will!

God is good all ways and always!

When you pray, don't beg God for answers. He doesn't want you begging; he wants you believing.

He's already provided everything that you need to live an abundant life here on earth.

I understand that you're taking a big risk to trust in someone for something you can't see.

It's almost easier and safer to say, "Well, if it's God's will, I will get my answer."

I will be healed, prosperous, happily married, etc.; whatever you are asking for.

When you believe that way, you don't have to put your faith out for it. You put everything on God.

If you don't get what you want, you can say it wasn't God's will for you to have it. You basically blame God, but it's you who failed.

God never fails us! He's provided everything that you need to get your prayers answered.

God will meet you where your faith is.

It is up to you to believe. He can't do that for you. He gave you everything else, including the faith to believe if you use it.

Don't be afraid to trust him; he never fails us, he never leaves us, and he never forsakes us.

CHAPTER 24

Now we're going to talk about money. Our father God owns everything, and we are heirs to all of it.

Jesus paid for our prosperity with his death, burial, and resurrection, just like he paid for forgiveness of our sins, healing, happiness, peace, etc.

2 Corinthians 8:9, KJV, says, "For ye know the grace of the Lord Jesus Christ, that though he was rich, yet for your sakes he became poor, that ye through his poverty might be rich."

That verse means you can be rich spiritually, physically, mentally, emotionally, and financially.

Matthew 6:33, KJV, says, "But seek ye first the kingdom of God and his righteousness, and all of these things will be added unto you."

If we seek God first in our lives, he supernaturally supplies our needs.

When God starts supplying your needs, he's not cheap! He's rather extravagant because he paves streets of gold.

CHAPTER 25

There is another law in the Bible. It's called seed, plant, and harvest.

God set up everything in our world to reproduce so that things could be replenished.

If he had not done that, all of the people would be gone, as would every plant and animal.

When a farmer plants a few seeds in the ground, they produce many thousands of seeds at harvest.

This is a system that God created.

If you sow, you reap, and you reap more than you sow.

We actually sow into our lives every day. We sow our words, money, attitude, and faith, for example.

When you speak, you are sowing seeds. Remember your words have power. Be careful what you say because you reap what you plant.

Galatians 6:7 (KJV) says, "You reap what you sow."

God is Good
All-Ways and Always!

If you are constantly sowing negativity, that's exactly what you will get.

By the same token, if you sow positivity, then that's what you get.

Your glass can be half empty or half full; it depends on how you look at it.

If it's half full, that shows that you are grateful. God blesses gratitude. You have to keep an attitude of gratitude to be happy and blessed.

If you have stinking thinking, your life will stink too, and people will respond to you with the same attitude.

If you are happy, positive, and grateful, your life will reflect that, and people will respond back likewise.

Now, regarding money. We are supposed to sow money into God's kingdom by supporting his ministries. Every ministry requires money to operate.

They are doing a job, working for God to reach lost souls.

We as Christians are supposed to support them.

At the very least we are to give 10 percent of our income as a tithe to the church.

When you give it with the right heart, God will bless the 90 percent that you have left, and it will go further than the 100 percent would have if you had kept it.

God says to test him in this.

Malachi 3:10, KJV, says, "Bring ye all the tithes into the storehouse, that there may be meat in my house, and prove me now herewith, saith the Lord of hosts, if I will not open you the windows of heaven, and pour you out a blessing, that there shall not be room enough to receive it."

The storehouse is wherever you are being spiritually fed. It is supposed to be the local church, but if you are being fed spiritually through an online ministry, then that is where you tithe.

When you tithe, God doesn't just drop money in your lap. God is not in our physical world; he's a spirit and operates in our spiritual world. He doesn't deal in money as we know it.

He blesses you to receive from sources here on earth. He anoints you with favor, ideas, gifts, and talents so that you can use them to produce all the physical and material things that you need.

He will inspire others to bless you, and he will work through other people to bring more business, increased profits, better deals, and even cash, etc.

Deuteronomy 8:18, KJV, says, "But thou shalt remember the Lord thy God: for it is he that giveth thee the power to get wealth, that he may establish his covenant which he swore unto thy fathers as it is this day."

God gives us power to get wealth. There isn't a first national bank of God here on earth. He can't give us money, but he can influence other people to do so.

He can bless our efforts to make money and give us new ideas and talents to make money.

In God's eyes, if you don't work, you don't eat, except for the disabled and others who are unable to work. If you are able to work and choose not to, God cannot bless your laziness.

2 Thessalonians 3:10, KJV, says, "...that if any would not work, neither shall they eat."

The real source of power is the anointing that God puts on us to produce wealth. With God being our source, our well will not run dry.

Abide by the law of seed, plant, and harvest, and God will give you an unending supply of wealth.

The blessings aren't just money or material things but include health, happiness, peace, love, joy, family, prosperity, protection, wisdom, and comfort, just to name a few.

CHAPTER 26

As a Christian, you should be blessed to be a blessing to others. I get excited about giving because I know that I am following God's law and his desire.

Money is supposed to flow through our hands to help others. The more that we give, the more God gives us to give. We will be blessed ourselves; you don't have to give it all away. God supplies abundant seeds for the Sower.

I always asked him, Who am I supposed to bless? God knows everyone's need, and I want to give to the one who is supposed to receive it.

I don't want any credit for it, and I always tell whoever I bless to give thanks to God.

I am just grateful to be a part of it. I want to give in to the kingdom. I want to serve God through giving because the goal is to reach lost souls. Its God's will that none should perish.

I never run short when I give. You can never outgive God. What you give will be multiplied back to you.

Don't be afraid to give, thinking that you are going to have to do without, because you will not.

I promise that this is the way that God's system of seed, plant, and harvest works.

I have lived and given according to this system.

Just like the law of faith, this law works if you use it.

Luke 6:38; KJV says, "Give, and it is given unto you, good measure, pressed together, shaken down, and running over, shall men give into your bosom. For with the same that you meet withal, it shall be measured to you again."

Now I'm not saying that you give to get, but I am saying that when you give with the right heart, you will get!

You cannot give grudgingly or because you are guilted into it.

You have to give with a happy heart. Be eager to give to God's ministry because of God. Because you want to see his work done here on earth so that souls can be saved.

God wants to prosper you because he loves you, just like faith for salvation and healing. You have to follow the law of seed, plant, and harvest to prosper.

God is Good
All-Ways and Always!

If a farmer doesn't plant a seed in the ground. When the harvest time comes, he cannot expect to receive anything back.

If you sow zero, then you reap zero.

This law is simple, but I understand it's not always easy. This is where faith comes in again. You have to trust God and believe that his words and promises are true.

I am telling you from my experience that they are true. You can trust him. This system does work, and it works every time.

I used to be reluctant to give because I was looking at what I made and then looking at my bills. I couldn't see how I was going to be able to afford to give.

So, for years I held back a little. What a huge mistake! What a lack of faith! God can't bless that, and he won't.

So, I struggled for years. Never really having enough. I didn't understand at the time that I was creating my own failure.

God cannot bless you if you don't use his laws and systems.

It's like laws that we have governing our lives here on earth. They are there for a reason, and if we break them, we lose in many ways, especially financially.

Traffic laws, for instance. There is a speed limit. If you follow it, you can drive through safely, and you will not get stopped and fined for breaking the law.

If you speed, you will most likely get stopped. Be given a ticket for a very high amount. Possibly get points on your license, which will cause your insurance to rise.

If you are going at an excessive rate of speed, you might be arrested and have to appear in court. That has additional expenses.

It would have been so much easier just to follow the law in the beginning.

You would be money ahead.

The same is true and even more so with God's laws. You will be more than just ahead if you follow them. You will be blessed!

If you don't give with a happy heart, God has no way of blessing you. His word says that you reap what you sow and more than you sow.

God is Good
All-Ways and Always!

It says, Give, and it will be given unto you good measure, pressed down, shaken together, and running over.

I can't help but think about brown sugar when I read that verse. It's talking about packing the blessings in, pressing them down, and shaking the vessel to get all that you can into it.

That's what God does for us if we follow his laws.

It won't only be money that is returned to you, but blessings come in many forms. You will receive peace, joy, love, happiness, marital blessings, and family blessings; everything in your life will be blessed.

Since I have decided to just do it. Just give without trying to figure it all out. I just give in faith, believing that God's word is true. God has blessed me immensely.

God is my source, and whatever I need, God supplies.

Philippians 4:19, KJV, says, "My God shall supply all of your need, according to his riches in heaven by Christ Jesus."

Through Jesus we received this promise. As children of God, we are not supposed to be living with scarcity and lack. We are supposed to live in abundance.

If you are not receiving riches, then you aren't using the laws that God created. You need to check yourself. Are you lazy, wasting money, not tithing, or using your money for things that God can't bless you for?

You have a part in receiving from God. Just because you read it in the Bible doesn't mean it automatically works for you.

You have to trust God, believe his word, and follow his laws. Have faith in him. Then he can and will bless you!

When I first started giving, like God instructed us to do. I barely had enough to pay my bills and didn't have money left over.

I decided to just do it and trust that God would hold up his end.

I can't say I was all in at first, but nevertheless I was going to give and be happy about giving.

I soon realized that it was working.

I gave just my 10% to start with, and I always had enough left over for everything else in my life.

So, I increased my giving. Not only did I give my tithe, I started giving an offering. I still had enough money left over. I soon realized that no matter how much more I gave, there was always money left over. It is a fact: you can't outgive God!

I needed a huge financial blessing from God. I put my faith in God for it.

We needed to sell a property that we owned, and we were in one of the worst economies ever.

I knew that the only way that it would sell was if God found a buyer. I started praying and believing that someone was going to walk into that place and want to buy it. Not only would they want to buy it, but they would also have the cash to buy it.

We didn't list the property because the economy was so bad. People were losing properties and going bankrupt at the time. We didn't think there was any use in listing it.

I decided that I would just trust God for it. I didn't see anything happening for the longest time.

I didn't stop believing, though, and I didn't stop giving.

One day I went to the property, and a man was there. He was an older gentleman. He said, I want to buy this building, and I have cash. So within 30 days it was his.

Wow! Only God! Hallelujah!!

CHAPTER 27

I'm not a perfect person, and I'm definitely not a perfect Christian, but God has given me a revelation from his word about healing and prosperity.

After I learned these principles, I put them to the test through faith, and they work!

I was in some situations that really left me no choice but to trust in Jesus' work on the cross. In my circumstances things looked extremely grim.

I could put my faith out for the miracles that I needed, or I could continue trying to figure it out on my own. I really didn't have anything to lose.

I was in desperate times. I could continue the way that I had always been, or I could go all in. With full faith in God, I expect my miracles.

I could ask in prayer and believe that I receive because his word says so.

God is Good
All-Ways and Always!

I could use faith the size of a mustard seed and speak to my mountain, and it would be removed.

I could use my words to save my life because life and death are in the power of our tongue.

I could trust that God will never leave me nor forsake me.

I could stand on the word that says by his stripes we were healed.

I could believe that he became poor so that we could be made rich.

I decided to just do it! I went all in with God; I put my faith into every word in the Bible. I believe without a doubt that it's all true. I've put it to the test, and it works.

God's laws work, faith as well as seed, plant and harvest.

My message to you is that God is good all-ways and always!

God is good in every area of your life, and he's good every day!

Put your faith and trust in him. Follow his laws of faith and seed, plant, and harvest.

Seek him and his righteousness, and every blessing will be given to you supernaturally.

God's word says this is true, and I know it is. I decided to use my faith and believe. I have received abundantly, and I continue to receive because I refuse to let go of his promises.

They are not just for me; they are for anyone who believes.

God loves you, and God is good all ways and always!

Made in the USA
Columbia, SC
26 June 2025